CONVICTION

IN
CUYAHOGA
COUNTY

Gladys

  May you be blessed
by the message of this
book, my father's testimony
of faith and eloquence.

       Jo Jo Weaver
       3/4/05

Property of ----.

Gladys C. Wilson
3660 Riedham Rd.
Shaker Hts, Ohio 44120

CONVICTION

IN
CUYAHOGA
COUNTY

A True Story
in Black
and White

Jo Jo Weaver

House of Jabez
SHAKER HEIGHTS, OHIO

Excerpt from ENCYCLOPEDIA OF SOUTHERN CULTURE, edited by William Ferris and Charles Reagan Wilson. Copyright © 1989 by the University of North Carolina Press. Used by permission of the publisher.

Excerpt from OUR LAWLESS POLICE by Ernest Jerome Hopkins, copyright 1931 by The Viking Press, Inc. Used by permission of Viking Penguin, a division of Penguin Group (USA) Inc.

Although the author and publisher have made every effort to ensure the accuracy and completeness of information contained in this book, we assume no responsibility for errors, inaccuracies, omissions, or any inconsistency herein. Any slights of people, places, or organizations are unintentional.

10 9 8 7 6 5 4 3 2 1

ISBN 0-9744215-4-5
LCCN 2003110905

ATTENTION CORPORATIONS, UNIVERSITIES, COLLEGES, AND PROFESSIONAL ORGANIZATIONS: Quantity discounts are available on bulk purchases of this book for educational, gift purposes, or as premiums for increasing magazine subscriptions or renewals. Special books or book excerpts can also be created to fit specific needs. For information, please contact House of Jabez, 16781 Chagrin Blvd., #247, Shaker Heights, OH 44120; (216) 751-9343; www.convictionincuyahoga.com.

This book is dedicated to
the memory of my father,
Joseph Weaver.

By example early in my life, he led me to appreciate
the English language and American history. Had
he not, the task of telling his story would have been
daunting.

TABLE OF CONTENTS

ACKNOWLEDGMENTS

There are so many people to thank for their contributions to this book: Dr. Judith G. Cetina of the Cuyahoga County Archives for permission to use her unpublished research on the old Cuyahoga County jail; Harry R. Esling, President, and Tim Bonness, Personnel Administrator, for history of the Midland Steel Products Company; Vern Sanford of Columbus, a storehouse of knowledge of the old Ohio Penitentiary, for arranging a private tour; and McCullough Williams, Chief of Legal Service at the Ohio Department of Rehabilitation and Correction, who arranged access to my father's prison file.

The dedicated professionals at the Cleveland Public Library, Cleveland State University Library, Western Reserve Historical Society, Cuyahoga County Archives, Akron Public Library, and at the Ohio Historical Society in Columbus made my research easier. I especially appreciate the assistance the University of Akron School of Law provided in the toughest part of my research tasks—tracking the story through the appellate court maze.

I thank my sister, Barbara Johnson, and longtime friends, Gladys Dunn and Charles Wagner. During the seven years when I was stalled in discouragement, they urged me never to give up. It took succinct direction, however, from Reverend Dr. Otis Moss, Jr., the pastor of Olivet Institutional Baptist Church, to jump-start this project in 2002. I cannot thank him enough.

Somehow the right persons (such as Reverend Moss) have appeared on the scene to play the exact role needed for this production at the time. None more right or recent than Penny Stetz whom I met at a public speaking organization meeting during the last phase of this project.

I was at my wit's end with a deadline to meet for final review of the text. Penny turned out to have the expertise I desperately needed. She came armed with computer skills equal to her editing ability, and suggestions that were right on target. All together, they made an immeasurable difference in getting me across the "finished" line. So last, but far from least, I thank Penny for the Godsend that she has been.

TO THE READER

The book title is descriptive of a quartet of men, black and white, with character traits as uncompromising as black or white. This story centers on one of them, Joseph Weaver, who was wrongly convicted of first-degree murder. Out of respect for him in particular, and so that you the reader can know him as he was, I have made considerable effort to adhere to the subtitle's claim of an unembellished presentation. Thus, the story is a biography journalistically presented and dramatically displayed against the social backdrop of America in the 1920s. Veracity is *Conviction*'s strength. Hence, the warts of early twentieth century journalism pop up throughout the text.

Nearly 4,000 years ago in Egypt, there lived another man named Joseph. He too lost his freedom undeservedly because of treachery. Later released and enlarged in social stature, he, the son of Jacob, said to the betrayers who ironically stood in need of his help:

"You intended to harm me, but God intended it for good to accomplish what is now being done, the saving of many lives."[1]

That sentiment of Old Testament Joseph resounds across the millennia. If the telling of this story accomplishes good in our time, then the harm Joseph Weaver endured in northern Ohio shall not have been in vain.

—Jo Jo Weaver

PROLOGUE

COUNTY OF CUYAHOGA
Cleveland, Ohio
June 3, 1938

My Dear Mr. Weaver:

How well do I recall the horrible experience which you were called upon to suffer, and I was one of those millions of persons acquainted with the case who was elated at the final outcome. Very often in my work here in the Prosecutor's office I have occasion to refer to the case of the State of Ohio vs. Joseph Weaver on certain matters of law. As long as there is a State of Ohio, that case will stand out as one of the beacon lights in our field of criminal law.

I can't tell you how much your kind letter has encouraged me. I am deeply gratified to know that there are those among us who appreciate the real significance of our war on crime. It has always been my philosophy, and it is the philosophy of justice, that all persons stand before the bar of justice equally. There should be no consideration of race or color or creed. If there were any abridgment of the rise of negroes [sic], I would be in the foremost ranks, fighting with all my strength; but just as I fight for what are our several rights, by the same token I ask for nothing more than that to which we are entitled. I ask not for license or indulgence, but the equal administration of the law.

Again may I thank you for your very kind letter.

Sincerely yours,
(signed) Norman S. Minor
Assistant Prosecuting Attorney

NSM:LF

1

* * *

Justice is the end of government, the end of Civil Society. It ever has been and ever will be pursued until it be obtained or until Liberty be lost in the Pursuit.

—the *Federalist*

Justice is exalted by awe and integrity; it is compromised by deceit and expediency. It is the trust of government by the innocent and the powerless.

Conviction in Cuyahoga County is a display of integrity stretched across the matrix of a compromised justice system. It centers on a black man's predicament during a time in our national history when the hand of justice was conceivably in its strongest interlock with the hand of bigotry.

Fortunately, other hands were at work—the hands of men who forged ahead on the high road towards that end acclaimed by the Federalist.

Justice when it serves the least well serves all best.

CHAPTER 1

THE BRIDGE

It was Christmas Day of 1935. Huge, knotty hands of a black man gripped the steering wheel of a dark blue Lincoln crossing the upper deck of the magnificently arched High Level Bridge. Joseph Weaver was on his way to Lakewood for a reason at odds with the nascent spirit of the day. Snowy gusts from the lake nearby buffeted the car as it rolled along the four-lane reinforced concrete and steel artery that spanned the Cuyahoga Valley. Through this natural divide of downtown Cleveland east and west, the Cuyahoga River meandered in its search for Lake Erie.

Christmas Eve editions of local newspapers had announced the death of Nathan Edward Cook the day before. His body would be laid to rest with Masonic rites the day after Christmas. Such news had shifted the holiday plans of hundreds of Ohioans towards paying their last respects to one of Cleveland's most colorful figures.

Joe Weaver had not known the highly regarded man for long—just eight years, the first three years, though, so compelling as to account for this journey from the East Side to the western suburb. So much was owed to Cook. Even the car Joe was driving; the man being mourned had a hand in it. Cook was present at a used-car dealership, along with his law partner, William Marsteller, when the powerful vehicle was picked out in 1933.

Cook's salesman friend, formerly a safety director for the city, led the three men to the used car department. First shown a very large, very powerful, very cheap—and very old—motorcar, Joe Weaver shook it off:

> "The people of Cleveland...[will] be expecting me to drive a little better car than that," he said to his friends.
>
> "What's your preference in color?" Marsteller asked.
>
> "Red," said Weaver. "But I ain't going to buy a red car. I want a dark car. I got a reason."
>
> Salesman Adams showed another car—a big, beautifully upholstered car with a fine paint job. It was dark blue and looked refined.
>
> "That's it," said Weaver, grinning broadly.
>
> "But, Joe," said Marsteller, "that'll take a lot of gasoline. It's a beauty, but—."
>
> "Mr. Marsteller, sir," said Weaver. "I didn't tell you, but I had an idea the other day. I figured that if I had a big car I might be able to go into business, driving for undertakers. I went around and talked to a lot of colored undertakers, and they said that if I had a nice big car I could drive in their funeral processions. I can get $10 a funeral."
>
> The argument ended right there. Joe bought his car. Then he looked out the window and frowned.
>
> "Do I have to take this car out right away?" he asked.
>
> "No," said Adams, grinning.
>
> "Then I think I'll leave it here till the ice gets off the street," said Weaver. "I don't want no fenders broke up on my car."[2]

The purchase was possible because Cuyahoga County had finally paid Joe half of the $12,000 awarded in scrip by the county commissioners. Earlier in the year, Nate Cook had successfully argued before the House of Representatives on Joe's behalf.

The year that was the worst of the Great Depression saw Cook's health begin a two-year decline that dragged the attorney down financially. By contrast, a healthy Joe Weaver was working as a longshoreman, and could afford T-bone steak at 23 cents a pound and eggs at 21 cents a dozen. With money left after buying the Lincoln, he gladly rendered assistance to his destitute friend shortly before Cook's death.[3]

Such sentiment towards Cook gave rise to a vow made on the morning of April 5, 1930. Joe showed up at Cook's office in the Leader Building downtown at 10:15. Dressed in a freshly pressed purple suit and a new tie, he stood resolutely in the reception area. Nathan Cook was in conference.

"Mr. Weaver's out here and he want to see you right away," the secretary said.

"Tell him to wait. I'll see him as soon as I can," Cook said, responding to the young lady's intercom buzz.

"But I can't let you see Mr. Cook now. You'll have to wait, Mr. Weaver," Cook's flustered secretary said. "He and Mr. Marsteller are busy with clients."

"But I've got to see them now and right away."

The intruder backed off.

Suddenly at 10:28, he rushed past the young woman's desk just as clients were coming out of Cook's office.

"Mistuh Cook, I don't want to seem to be forcing myself in, suh," Joe said, looking apologetic.

"I don't know whether you-all remember, but it's just one year ago today that I walked out of Judge White's courtroom a free man. And I've made up my mind that every year so long as we three live, at 10:30, the very hour I was freed, I'm going to be here with you both in this office holdin' your hand."[4]

The propriety of the vow was affirmed 17 days later when stunning news stopped Joe Weaver in his tracks. Some reporters called it Red Monday, others the Easter Monday fire. However labeled, April 21, 1930, was a day of unimaginable horror for the hapless mass of humanity locked up in the Ohio Penitentiary. Whether by newsprint or radio that week, Joe was drawn into the perils of that scene in the state capital.

It was worse than war in the judgment of State Senator Thomas W. Jones of Pomeroy. The veteran was near the prison when the alarm sounded and had watched as the firemen went in.

"I saw some of the fighting in the Meuse-Argonne and at St. Mihiel," he declared. "Today was far worse. We had a chance overseas. The prisoners had none."[5]

"War, don't tell me it's like that war. I seen both," snarled a burly inmate [later in reflection]. "You got legs and can run in war. Here all you can do is go crazy and yell for God to open the doors."[6]

The men had returned to the cells after the 4:30 evening meal, the door to the cell block locked behind them.[7]

Each range had two keys to unlock all cells on that range but not cells of any other range.

Each cell block had two guards, whose duties, after prisoners were locked up, were to patrol ranges, one taking the upper and the other the lower ranges.[8]

Charles Oliver, a convict from Toledo, described his ordeal to a *United Press* correspondent.

"You can't imagine the horror of it!

"I was on the fourth tier of Section H, directly beneath the place where the fire broke out.

"The fire swept towards the confined men like some charging monster. It was upon us before we scarcely realized what was happening. The flames were sweeping in great sheets along the cell block and it began to get hot.

"There were four of us in our cell. We were scared. I'll admit, scared half to death. We started screaming to be turned loose—to be let out of that cell.

"We yelled and yelled at the guards to come and let us out. Some of the boys who were yelling didn't use nice language, but we wanted to get out.

"It seemed as if we were going to be roasted alive. It got hotter and hotter. I hope I never go to hell if it's that hot.

"We finally hit on the idea of turning on the water tap in our cell. We let it run wide open and pretty soon the floor was covered with water."

Prisoners all over the cell blocks were screaming, putting their faces down in the water, rolling around in it, splashing it on one another.

"We had given up. We expected to die, lying there in the water with the flames cracking all around us. Then at last a couple of prisoners came along and knocked the lock off our cell door with a sledge hammer.

"We dashed into the hall—a hall of flame. We helped knock the locks off three other cells and helped the men get out.

"Before we could get out to safety, the flames were scorching us, singeing the hair off our heads.

"It's my opinion the fire started from a short circuit. They've been having trouble with the lights. They were all the time going on and off for no apparent reason."[9]

The old wooden cell block on West Spring Street had stood its ground since 1876, kindling for the fire of disputed origin. By 1930, the antiquated prison confined more than 4,300 men, though built for fewer than 1,500.[10]

Six ranges made up of 17 four-man cells extended north and south from the western end of the Administration building for some 300 yards.[11]

At 5:39, someone outside the 96-year-old limestone front on Spring Street rang up the Columbus fire department. The call went out and the Ohio National Guard responded from Columbus, Lancaster, Chillicothe, and a dozen other points in the vicinity of the state capital.[12]

Eight pumpers and 135 to 140 firemen were soon pouring water from twenty-three lines of hose. Some 200 city policemen arrived about the same time as the firemen, and not long afterwards federal troops from Fort Hayes and hundreds of National Guardsmen and naval reserves joined them.[13]

Fire was spreading from west to east, blazing up more than 25 feet. About 5:40 p.m., *Columbus This Week* editor Ray W.

Humphreys was driving past the penitentiary on West Spring Street when he saw smoke billowing from the structure.

> [Humphreys] parked his automobile and climbed to the top of an oil tank overlooking the west side of the prison, where the burning cellblocks were located. There he took [a] picture at about 5:45, just as the fire department was directing its first stream of water onto the blaze.[14]

Warden Preston E. Thomas was sitting on the porch that overlooked the street when the fire started. He shouted an order to his daughter to call the fire department.

The first alarm was turned in about 5:50, about the same time as a guard on the south wall saw the smoke and fired his rifle to attract attention.

William Baldwin and Thomas Little, in the prison's guard room a half hour before their six o'clock shift, reacted to a call of "fire." The warden ordered his guards to go and unlock the gate so the fire department could get in, take the keys, and go to the cell block.

Guards Baldwin and Little took the keys that opened up the cell doors. They made their way through E and F dormitories. The fire was rapidly spreading from new cell blocks I and J to the old ones, G and H. The two men of contrasting girths hustled to the door that led to the upper tiers. They found it locked. They demanded that the guard on duty with the keys open the door. They could hear the prisoners screaming, "Open those God-damned doors!" Little and Baldwin implored John Watkinson, a pudgy little man, 55, with a whining voice and a rough-edged, gray mustache, to open the doors, but their comrade stood firm on ceremony.

Against the screams and curses he informed them he had orders to let nobody out, and that if he disobeyed instructions, he probably would be suspended.[15]

"To hell with the orders! Open up or we'll bust the door in," said Baldwin while his slim partner chimed, "Open the door!"

Seventy-one-year-old John Hall, lean, sparse, and gray, was captain of the night guard. He entered the block behind Baldwin and Little.

"Wait a minute. Don't open the door," Hall commanded.

"Captain, I'm ready to open it when you say so," said Watkinson, unperturbed by the barks of crazed men.

Rather than argue any more, Little wrested the key from Watkinson. He along with Baldwin unlocked the lower tier cells, then rushed around looking for something with which to ram in the door.

"For God's sake, let's get to those other men," shouted an inmate the duo had released. He and others tried beating down the doors.

Part of the woolen mill nearest the burning block caught fire repeatedly. Firemen had the two-front task of fighting flames and frenzied convicts. Locked behind bars of the old west wing, helpless prisoners shrieked, choked, and roasted to death in the fire that invaded their cells.[16]

> Rescuers… found many victims with their hands grasping the bars near the floor, while others had their heads covered with bed clothing in an effort to escape the suffocating fumes, or to shut out the horror of death. One convict brought from a cell had stabbed himself to death. Another slashed his throat with a razor….
>
> Once under way the fire spread with amazing rapidity, sweeping up over the roof. The men in the upper tiers of cells were burned to death while those lower down suffocated….[17]
>
> Their end was sudden. The dry wood and straw mattresses burned like powder and the men could only beat their fists against the iron bars and walls.
>
> The fire spread to the fifth range next, while the trapped men shrieked and screamed for help.
>
> Not many of this range were left alive when the firemen arrived. It was all but impossible for any rescuers to reach them.

Prisoners who got out into the yard dashed time after time into the building, to return with a blackened body in a blanket, with one man at each corner. They worked side by side with guards, firemen and policemen, often until they dropped.

Many fought hardest to get their pals out of the trap and were badly burned but always they tried to return to the task. Blacks and whites worked alike, with shouts and screams of agony ringing into their ears. First a burst of flame, then a thick cloud of smoke filled the cell block and hung over the yard, thick and biting.

Through this cloud the fire showed through the barred windows. Firemen threw water until the yard was a foot deep in water in places. Now and then a puddle would run toward a body on the ground, covered with a blanket. A prisoner would try to drag the body to a dryer spot.

"It's no use—he's gone," someone would say. Then they'd go about looking after the living.

Nurses and trusties met the rescuers near the door with tin cups of coffee. All the while they were in danger from falling walls. More than once a shout of warning sent the crowds flying over wire fences and down into puddles of water.

One man flung his brother over his shoulder and fought his way through the fire only to find he was bearing a body. That body joined the silent ranks—row after row of them—side by side on the wet ground.

One guard, his clothing afire, handed his pistol to one convict and his keys to another. Convicts swung axes and sledge hammers and crowbars. One, with a grappling hook he had fixed up, tried to make a rope fasten to the top of the upper cell windows. A big Negro, with his head wrapped in a white bandage, was screaming inside. He couldn't save him....[18]

Guard Little and his partner opened as many cells as they could, but on the sixth range the heat had caused the locks to stick.

Little, unlocking the cells, saved at least 200 men and worked until his clothing was in flames. He tossed the keys to a trusty before other trusties carried him out of the blazing structure.

By this time, the cell bars were red hot on the two upper tiers....The heat was intense and suffocating smoke filled the building.

Roy Renftle and "Tex" Bevais of Cleveland and Charles Sheflet of Lima, armed with crowbars and sledges, attacked the bars and cleared the way for the other rescuers. Renftle smashed the locks while Sheflet—after Guard Little tossed him the keys—worked just as desperately.

The fire...raced through the structure, burning the straw mattresses. Flames darted from one cell to the next. Shelving on the walls and the four chairs allowed to each cell caught [fire] quickly....

It was but an instant before the roof caught fire and from that moment forward, most of the helpless men were doomed....

Everyone on the fifth and sixth ranges died in the flames, screaming and beating frantically at the doors of their cells and begging guards to [either] shoot them or give them the keys.

One tale was simply told. It was a note pinned by one prisoner to his shirt front, neatly written in lead pencil.

"Gus Socka," it said at the top. "Notify John Dee.... Cincinnati." Socka was dead when his body was removed.[19]

A trusty, who had helped in the rescue work from the moment the blaze was discovered, said later the men screamed for help for twenty minutes before the doors to their cells were opened.

One of the prisoners claimed that the day guard had said when begged to give up the keys he couldn't unlock the doors because somebody might go over the wall and he, the guard, "would be responsible."[20]

Liston G. Schooley, formerly Cleveland city councilman who [was] serving a five-year sentence for participation in a land graft deal, was in the deputy warden's office when the fire started, he said.

"I looked out of the window and saw smoke," said Schooley. "A nurse yelled, 'The G and H block is on fire!' I grabbed a telephone...."

The vicious fight with fear-crazed convicts bent on letting the entire pen go up in flames was described by Fire Chief C. W. Osburn, whose battalion was one of the first in the grounds.

"We were surrounded by frantic convicts," he said. "They said we were not trying to put out the blaze and were mad with horror at seeing their comrades die like rats in a trap.

"Finally a fire hose was cut. I saw a convict with a knife in his hand running away from the hose...."

Capt. John Hall said that he was in the guardroom when the fire broke out.

"I told the prisoners to open the windows of their cells because of the heavy smoke," said Hall.

Lives of the convict rescuers were repeatedly imperiled by crashing walls and debris. They halted momentarily but always pushed forward again.

They refused to be stopped by solid walls of flame. Cursing and screaming they pushed their way thru flames...many never came back.

Some tore keys from reluctant guards and unlocked doors in the cells of their doomed companions. Some carried axes grabbed from the hands of weary firemen. Some used only their bare strength which was increased to superhuman proportions as the gasping wails of dying comrades penetrated the crackling flames.

Negro convicts appeared frequently in the rescue squads. Avidly they clenched stretchers and refused to be detered [sic] from their errands of mercy by falling mortar and roaring fire.

Smoke grimed, gasping, handkerchiefs tied over their mouths, they stumbled from exits of the burning cell block, the limp forms of victims hanging from their shoulders.[21]

Of 262 men on the fifth and sixth ranges of G and H, all but 13 perished. A couple hundred policemen swooped upon the scene to flank the fire fighters. Shortly thereafter, hundreds of national guardsmen, naval reservists, and federal troops from Fort

Hayes joined forces with the firemen. The call went out to every available physician when the magnitude of the disaster became apparent. The conflagration was reaching for a record in such disasters. News of the fire flashed across the state capital. Thousands in automobiles and on foot rushed to the vicinity of the big prison to stand in awe. Friends of the prisoners cried out in anguish. Family members fainted. Doctors, nurses, ministers, and Red Cross and Salvation Army workers streamed in throughout the night to care for the injured and perform other services. Police escorts were needed to get them through the pressing throng gathered outside the walls. Nearly a dozen large army trucks from the Ohio National Guard pulled into the yard and exited with loads of dead bodies peeled off stacks in the prison courtyard. They made round trips to the state fairgrounds, the temporary morgue for the charred bodies. Fifty undertakers readied the remains for burial.

> While firemen fought the flames, that part of the woolen mills nearest the burning cell block took fire repeatedly and some convicts, in a frenzy, battled with the firemen who were trying to save the building and who finally succeeded in doing so.
> The burned cell block held the company known as the "Rough Riders," those who were either crippled or unable to work; the machine shop company; one idle company; the woolen mills company; the cotton mills company; and the print shop....
> Prisoners in dormitories and in cells away from the burning wing were quieted by guards when there was no danger, or released to stand about in the prison yard, dazed and stunned by the disaster. The few who were able to save any of their pitiful belongings—a battered traveling bag, some pictures, or possibly a book—piled them among the dead, and wandered about inquiring for this or that acquaintance or cell mate, only to be told—too often: "Old Larry is dead," or "He's gone, too...."[22]

> Some men lay on the cell floors, their lifeless hands gripping the bars. Others were on their cots with wet blankets.... Two of the dead men had cut their throats, driven to suicide by the terror...

as the flames mowed their prison mates to death back of the prisoning [*sic*] bars.

Other bodies showed bullet holes, mute sign probably of some guard's gun spelling death for a desperate prisoner. Still others were twisted in postures of madness. Others showed evidence of heavy blows about the body and face, marks of the mad struggle for escape among the doomed men.[23]

Among the expired in "K" cell block was an Ironton man, only a few hours into serving time for abandoning his children.

Unlike Clevelander Charles Greene who fought his way down the red hot steel corridors through blinding smoke to carry out 42 dead men, some inmates tried to create further havoc.

They taunted the firemen, cut hoses, and started fires in other parts of the prison.

Dying convicts were given whisky by guards as they lay in the enclosure of the penitentiary....

There was "One-Armed" Pete—with one good arm; the other had been shattered by machine-gun bullets. That arm pulled man after man out of the inferno, then it brought out his cellmate, his buddy, and Pete "came apart." He was trying to rub his own eyes out when guards took him....[24]

The cotton mill caught fire about an hour after the west cell block broke into flames. Prisoners told firemen to let it burn and made threats. The firemen continued to fight the fire under guard.

Militiamen, army regulars, and police were ordered to shoot to kill at the first sign of resistance.

Once when the clamor within the big yard had shrilled to a pitch that indicated dangerous fury, the bayonets of the military glinted and moved forward in formation into the darkness....[25]

Flood lights were turned into the prison yards late [that] night. Under the blazing lights, soldiers and national guardsmen aided prison guards in driving the loose convicts into their cells. The work was arduous, for most of the prisoners were milling about and paying little attention to orders.

> By some irony of chance, all the prisoners awaiting execution
> in death row escaped [the fire]. When the blaze menaced their
> cells, they were transferred to the solitary confinement section....[26]

In all, 322 men perished in the deadliest prison conflagration the nation had ever seen. Indeed, the vow Joe Weaver had established with Nate Cook and Bill Marsteller was affirmed by the tragedy of Red Monday.

The annual handshake ritual was not always easily kept, as the very next year proved when April 5th fell on Easter Sunday. Eight years earlier, Joe had joined a church choir. His sonorous voice bottomed the spirituals, "anthemized spirituals" such as *I'll Never Turn Back* by black composer Nathaniel Dett, and anthems the choir sang. Problematic for Joe, a rule required the choir member's presence in the stand by 10:15 on Sunday mornings. Joe showed up at his former attorney's office two days before Easter to explain his dilemma.

"I don't know quite what I'm going to do, Mistuh Cook."

"Don't worry," Cook replied. "I'll come to your church."[27]

On the first day of every week, huge crowds flocked to an old red limestone of Gothic pointed arches and twin turreted towers on East 37th Street. Once a Jewish synagogue, it now served as a Baptist church in the part of the city that was absorbing blacks from the South.[28]

Among the Easter Sunday throng of early arrivals at Zion Hill were two men of physical contrast. One, white and stocky, was dressed in his everyday business suit; the other, black and tall, was robed to sing. The two men sat on a pew in the rear of the sanctuary. The awaited moment had to be exactly right.

Ten-thirty, the right moment, brought them to their feet, hands locked in a firm handshake. Then, as one looked on, the other walked the center aisle to the choir stand. Joe Weaver was satisfied. His vow was intact.[29]

Zion Hill Baptist Church. Sunday morning service—1940s photo.

Photographer unknown

CHAPTER 2

THE PUSH
AND THE PULL

The Lincoln rolled off the upper level of the double-deck bridge, the driver somber and reflective—and alone. The woman he had married in 1919 was nowhere to be found when the court granted him a divorce in 1934. The grounds: her willful absence for more than four years.

"Maybe she did not expect her husband to come back," the domestic relations court judge had said after hearing that the plaintiff's wife had sold all his clothes while he was away in Columbus.[30]

Joe had married Orrie Williams in Waynesboro, Georgia, where he was born on December 7, 1893, on the younger end of 13 children. It could be that he met her early in life in a one-room schoolhouse, or in a church meeting where Joe's father, a former slave, preached the gospel. Just as likely, his path crossed Orrie's in a cotton field. While strong, gently sloped shoulders humbled the big man's appearance, the tall, brown-skinned woman who became his wife looked as if royal tribal blood coursed through her veins. There was, however, nothing regal about picking corn and cotton in the hot Georgia sun.

The Weavers were sharecroppers, workers in an economic scheme that came on the heels of slavery. After the Civil War, the plantation system had begun to crumble. Landowners were left abruptly without labor, and emancipated slaves without means for launching new lives. The much ballyhooed "forty acres and a mule" was far beyond the freed men's horizon, and in many cases, their desire. Freedom of mobility was preferred over re-attachment to any farmland. Damning caution, former slaves and their offspring left the poverty of the rural South in droves. Ten thousand went to Liberia, a few thousand to Haiti.

A vast number migrated to urban America. Not surprisingly, they were ill-equipped to live in such a setting. Thousands of others, however, stayed on the planter's soil to become enmeshed in an economic net commonly called sharecropping. The crop-lien system was installed to benefit the landowner by ensuring the next year's labor supply. On paper the system looked fair. The landowners and merchants supplied the land, tools, animals, and shelter. The farmhands provided the labor, expecting a share-and-share-alike division of the crop at the end of the year, with the cropper's expenses deducted from his share. How it worked in reality was quite different.

> As soon as the young Negro marries he begins working for some land owner [sic] under these conditions. He never has enough in cash ahead to buy everything in the way of food and clothing that he and his family need; therefore he must go to the landlord for these things. The landlord either has a plantation store or has arrangements made with the nearby village or small town store to credit the Negro and charge the account to the landlord. In the majority of cases the Negro is uneducated and unable to keep an accurate account of what he buys. He simply trusts the landlord. Even if he has an education and keeps an account, he is not permitted to compare his books with those kept by the landlord. The account as kept by the latter is the one the settlement is based on at the end of the year when the crop is sold. If the Negro has bought five bacon middlings for 40 cents a pound he is charged up with fifteen or so, and at a much higher price than the regular store price. He may have bought a barrel of flour, but he must pay for two or three at extortionate prices. He

may have ploughed in rocky fields bare-footed to save having to buy more than one pair of shoes, but he finds at the end of the year his memory has played a trick and he has really, according to the store account, enjoyed the luxury of two pair [*sic*] or three pairs of healthy [*sic*] priced shoes. His wife may have gone through the year with two cheap calico dresses and find in December that she has, in fact, dressed quite sumptuously during the year—according to the infallible store record....[31]

In a 1930s interview conducted by the Federal Writers Project, an adjunct of the Works Project Administration, former slave Henry Blake recounted an experience similar in its cynicism.

After freedom, we worked on shares a while. Then, we rented. When we worked on shares, we couldn't make nothing—just overalls and something to eat. Half went to the white man, and you would destroy your half, if you weren't careful. A man that didn't know how to count would always lose. He might lose anyhow. The white folks didn't give no itemized statement. No, you just had to take their word. They never give you no details. They just say you owe so much. No matter how good account you kept, you had to go by their account and—now, brother, I'm telling you the truth about this—it's been that way for a long time. You had to take the white man's word on notes and everything. Anything you wanted you could get, if you were a good hand. If you didn't make no money, that's all right; they would advance you more. But you better not try to leave and get caught. They'd keep you in debt. They were sharp. Christmas come, you could take up twenty dollars in somethin'-to-eat and much as you wanted in whiskey. You could buy a gallon of whiskey—anything that kept you a slave. Because he was always right and you were always wrong if there was a difference. If there was an argument, he would get mad and there would be a shooting take place.[32]

Such chicanery seeded a mistrust of whites that lodged in the psyche of many southern blacks going North. Just as forceful as the economic exploitation were the affronts of disenfranchisement and segregation, the denial of citizen's rights on railroads, in streetcars, parks, and other public places, the terror of lynching and cross-burning by night, and the inequities in the educational systems. Humiliation was the thread woven through the fabric of southern black life. The NAACP took up the summary cause for the exodus with the federal Department of Justice. The New York office passed on to the Department a letter it had received.

The letter well answers the question as to why our people are leaving the South. It is as follows:

"Gentlemen: As I cannot read or write, I got a friend to write this. Never in school in my life, I worked on this man's (name withheld for federal action) farm all my life. Never did get a cent for my labor until I ran away. I am 35 years old. All we Negroes got to eat was cornbread and bacon and a few clothes. Four to 10-12 lived in a one-room shack. His overseers carried stick, whip and gun. They whipped children, women and men. They would make men and women strip their clothes down and get on their knees and sometimes tie them to a plow and whip them from 25 to 100 lashes at a time. You dare to ask for money or anything else! Where I am now, I am getting paid, once every week, and buying a house. My wife has a job also and, the children are going to school.

"I did not know before there was living, in the world, for Negroes. If I send you my name would it be any danger of them carrying me back to Georgia? My own children never ever got any clothing scarcely there.

"The overseer (in Georgia) ordered all the boys last March or the first of April, 15 years and down to leave off their pants and stay in their shirt-tails until cold weather, about the first of November. So what do you think of the Negroes leaving? Shirts generally come to the top of the knees. Girls could not hide their nakedness. Overseers seduced any young girl they wanted and parents could not help themselves. I would send my name but I don't want to go back to that farm. I never did commit a crime."

The white man accused of peonage lives in Atlanta, Ga., and has a farm from which many of our people are reported to have fled in recent months.

In connection with the estimated northern migration of 500,000 Negroes in a year, South Carolina's expenditures on the white and colored children are offered in evidence...as one of the chief causes disposing colored people to leave the South. The figures published by South Carolina's Department of Education shows that ten times as much was spent on white as on Negro children, although the Negro population at the 1920 census exceeded the white population. The South Carolina educational statistics, covering the years 1922-1923, as compiled by...the state supervisor of rural schools, and published in the Charleston News and Courier of October 31, 1923, are as follows:

...Total education expenditure—White, $10,024,046.96; Negro, $1,119,142.62. Transportation of pupils—White, $8, 903.94; Negro, $3.00. Libraries—White, $1,310.02; Negro, $6.69....[33]

In the eyes of many in the South, the grass understandably had a greener hue the farther on the other side of the Mason Dixon line it lay.

"Pull up and leave what you cannot bring and begin life over where civilized people are. It may be hard for the older ones but it will be the making of the younger ones...."[34]

Such an exhortation was issued regularly in northern black newspapers such as the *Gazette* in Cleveland. Every Saturday, beginning in 1883, Harry Clay Smith's four-page watchdog of race matters hit the streets with recurring themes. Some blacks took that advice westward during Reconstruction and established communities such as Nicodemus, Kansas, when met with hostility from white settlers of the frontier.

The primary challenge, then, that black migrants faced in any direction on the compass was to find a hospitable place in which to set down roots and thrive. Some fresh off the plantations merely moved to other rural areas of the South, small towns with colorful names such as New Africa, New Rising Sun, Slabtown, and Promised Land established by others of the race. Thousands of others descended upon the South's increasingly industrialized cities where the wages were high when stacked against farm change. In those cities, colored cocoons already existed. Memphis had Beale Street; Atlanta "Sweet Auburn." Black institutions, political activity, recreation, and freedmen's schools furthered the draw of city life. Still, the people of African origin were in a region of the country where skin color rigidly defined boundaries.

> "See that fellow," a white laborer said to a *United Press* correspondent in Atlanta. "He's getting 60 cents an hour. Why should that black man be getting 60 cents an hour for carrying the United States mail while white men are out of jobs?"[35]
>
> Whenever black people left "their own" areas, they were confronted at every turn by demeaning and often debilitating restrictions. Housing was segregated not only by custom… but by law. The few blacks who could afford it were born in black hospitals…. They went to black schools. When they rode public transportation, they sat in the black section in the rear. If they wanted to drink, eat, or go to the toilet, they might be lucky enough to find facilities reserved for them; otherwise they had to do without. Parks, beaches, golf courses, tennis courts, and swimming pools excluded them…. If they ran afoul of the law, they were sworn on separate-but-equal Bibles and, if convicted by usually all-white juries, were sentenced by white judges to segregated jails. When they died, they were embalmed in black funeral parlors (one of the most promising businesses for the black bourgeoisie) and buried in black cemeteries.[36]

A sizable number that vacated the farms preferred to go north the way the crow flies. They skipped altogether the usual route through the South's urban districts. But in the colder latitudes, they found themselves welcome only in certain parts. Outlying areas and small towns of the Northeast shared the keep-them-out sentiment of the West.

Against this social and economic backdrop, Joe and Orrie's routine was hard work in the fields. Somehow in 1922, after three years of marriage—and a miscarriage or two—the couple managed to disentangle themselves from the sharecropping web and leave Burke County. They chose the usual route, making Georgia's largest city their first stop. Seventy-five cents was a good day's pay in Atlanta to someone who had rarely seen cash in hand.

Segregated though the city was, it offered Joe a couple of opportunities to latch onto. By day he worked in construction. In the evening he took classes at school. The stay was brief in Atlanta, little more than a tag-up before take-off for a more promising urban center. In the fall of 1922, the Weavers boarded a train for one of the several northern cities where Henry Ford was paying $5.00 a day in auto plants.

European immigration to America had been curtailed after the Great War. A national search was on for cheap labor. Northern industry picked up the welcome mat that had been along the Atlantic coast and laid it at the Mason-Dixon line. This hunt for industrial labor coincided with the diminishing need for farmhands in the South. Farm mechanization had been increasing since the turn of the century with an accelerating effect on black migration. In Cleveland, Harry Smith justified the swelling presence of blacks in northern cities. The owner-editor said in his tabloid that was more opinion than news:

> Georgia and Alabama have grown desperate as a result of the emigration of our people from those states and have turned to their legislatures for greatly desired relief. It is a vain effort, a waste of time.
>
> When the people of that and other southern states awaken to the fact that they have simply got to treat our people in that section of the country as human beings, and Americans, and do it, then and only then will the emigration cease largely. All the laws this side of Jericho will not stop the emigration just as long as they keep up their hellish mistreatment of Afro-Americans in the South.[37]

Pushed by the ravages of the boll weevil, floods, unemployment after the collapse of an exploitative tenancy-sharecropping system, and surging racism, black people were eager to escape the South. But not until these factors were combined with the pull of better jobs and a better life, especially in the war-stimulated, labor-starved industries of northern cities, did a mass migration begin. The move was facilitated by black newspapers like the *Chicago Defender*, by labor recruiters offering free train tickets, and by word of mouth.[38]

Black migration outran the South's farm mechanization. During the three and a half years before the summer of 1923, 229,800 blacks took Georgia off their minds. In just the first six months of 1923, 77,000 blacks, in contrast to 29,500 whites, left the farms. Farm labor was down an estimated 70,700 workers in just the Peach State alone. Nearly 47,000 farm dwellings were left vacant. There were 55,522 plows idle, with an estimated 30 acres to the plow.[39]

Numbers like these drove Georgia lawmakers to produce a bill to check the migration of Negroes and other farm laborers. It stated that any person or concern caught soliciting labor in Georgia for other states should be found guilty of a felony and punished by a prison term of three to seven years. The bill took aim at interlopers known as labor agents.[40]

So great was the need for plant workers in the North that such scouts regularly crossed the Mason-Dixon to entice unskilled farmhands north to greener pastures. One who nibbled happily was Pompeii Lovejoy.

"What you doin' up here, Mister Sam?"

A familiar voice called to Sam Whitmire in the shuffling crowd of 30,000 that had cheered the Brooklyn team's victory over the Cincinnati Reds at Ebbett's Field.

That Sunday in 1923 Pompeii had not seen his fellow Georgian in 10 years, not since he laid mortar and stone for a chimney added to the white man's bungalow in Rome. Pompeii told his former employer that labor agents hunting for help for a brickyard at Newburgh, New York, had appeared before the Masonic lodge in his home town, touting the joys of life in New York. He said the labor agent had paid travel expenses for him and sixteen others who left Rome with him. Before they knew it, they were in Newburgh making $6.00 a day for rolling bricks in wheelbarrows.

Pompeii said after a few months up the Hudson, he met another labor agent who was seeking bricklayers for a firm of New York contractors. This agent told him how good he'd have it living in Brooklyn: steam heat; electric lights in an apartment; public schools where his children could sit with rich white folk's children. Eleven dollars a day to lay bricks eight hours a day, with a half day off every Saturday. And the agent showed him how he also could keep his family busy making money.

"I get $66.00 a week, and am never out of work," Pompeii boasted, "and I get treated just like white folks up here. You know, down home I never woulda been let in the grandstand to see a ball game—Ida been out on the bleachers, rain or shine. And if you go with me tonight, I will show you how they treat us in the white folk's church up here." [41]

Pompeii bragged that his wife earned $18 weekly ironing in a laundry and his sixteen-year-old daughter $15 each week as a maid, making about as much in tips. He said three members of his family took home $400 every time the moon was full and they were "able to bank $200 every month after living as well as white folks do down South." [42]

More and more, the "let down your buckets where you are" philosophy of educator Booker T. Washington was being supplanted by the practice of blacks who preferred to take up their beds and walk. [43]

* * *

The Lincoln turned left onto a winding street in Lakewood, destined for a yellow brick house. Inside the large abode, mourners filed past an opened casket and offered sympathy to the widow and three sons.

Nathan Cook, whose father was Jewish and mother Czechoslovakian, had died at 53 from heart disease after living a vibrant life, part of it spent in an illustrious political career as secretary to the mayor.

> Those wise in politics say that there has been no more powerful mayor's secretary in more than two decades. He was suave, tactful, as well as forceful. He "steered" people who visited the mayor's office. Through his position he became known to thousands of Clevelanders as a "good man to have in your corner...."[44]

Few if any viewing the remains knew better than Joe Weaver just how good a "corner" man he had been; for Cook, who never lost a client to the electric chair, was at his best in a life-and-death arena.

> Though noted for his power, Cook had been highly regarded for another distinguishing trait: loyalty so immutable even his political foes saluted it.
>
> Even the most partisan observers of the Cleveland political scene acknowledged that he demonstrated human loyalty and devotion in a degree few men seem capable of doing.
>
> It was axiomatic for a long time in city politics that it was good to have Nate Cook as a friend and pretty tough to have him against you.[45]

Mourning throughout the large house was alloyed with light-hearted recollections of Cook's quirky mannerisms: the spectacular bluster with which he once served his political mentor, Harry L. Davis; and a sports fanaticism over the decades that stood out in the city reputedly raving mad about baseball even in 1903.

Cook was officially the City's Number One Fan. Rabid loyalty to the hometown team had won for him that title and regular caricature in the newspapers over captions such as: *So Crazy Over Baseball He Gets in the Streets and Makes Public Speeches to Fans.* Enthusiasts, who knew a dyed-in-the-wool fan when they saw one, maintained that the holder of such a title should be a rootin', tootin', rantin', raving son-of-a-gun, and a natural born leader of his fellow rooters. Requirements that Cook, the noisiest rooter in the ballpark, easily met. Every afternoon that the baseball team was in town, he was in the stands sporting his flat top straw hat and ever-present cigar. No less loyal to an eighth place team was Cook than to the winner of the 1920 World Series. When the Indians pulled off a bases-loaded home run and an unassisted triple play at the expense of the Brooklyn Dodgers to win the Series, Nate Cook leaped with the wildest of fans. Whether organizing an amateur sandlot support group in 1905 or attending every World Series game but two in thirty years, Cook manifested devotion to the sport. As Number One Fan, he competed with other champion rooters from all parts of the nation for the prize of a gold medal pass that admitted the winner to every major league ballpark in the country.[46]

Every Naps game saw the familiar figure about town tear open his shirt, get red in the face, and lead his fellows in the wildest rooting the city had ever seen. When Cook cut loose, it was infectious. He could get 'em going as no other Cleveland booster could. From his private box along the third base line, his yell could be heard all over the stands.

When the 1913 team was a contender for the American League pennant, the city was wild with pennant fever. Great noontime crowds congregated on Public Square.

"This is Cleveland's year," [Cook] shouted noon in and noon out. "Get aboard that Payne Avenue car over there and hustle out to Somers' Park, and root like you never rooted before! We need every bit of rooting we can get to pull this old pennant over."

And when the race was over with the pennant going to Philadelphia, this fellow still was rooting.

"We'll get that flag next year—or bust," was his winter cry.

Business can go to blazes for all Nate cares when there's a ballgame on tap. But in spite of his close attention to baseball he's a keen business man, and has built up a business that enables him to spend his afternoons rooting at the ball park....[47]

There may be a greater fan in the world than Cook, concluded a *Cleveland Press* sports writer, but "this is his claim to fame: He always pays his way, refuses to take passes—and never knocks the home team."[48]

Even outside the sports section, the feisty Clevelander was regular grist for the news mill. He had resigned from the position of private secretary to the mayor at the end of 1917 to practice law. In his new career, he chose to champion the poor and the powerless. The indefatigable Cook was doing just that in 1930 as a guest on the radio. A fellow member of the Cuyahoga County Bar Association was asking him questions. The subject of the Bar's educational series was *The Third Degree*.

The interview centered on a newlywed who had faced a murder charge in the death of his young bride in Cleveland's Little Italy. Cook had served as co-counsel for the young man whose death was officially ruled the suicide of a confessed murderer who feared standing trial.

> Tony Colletti was the youth who hanged himself in County Jail while awaiting trial for the murder of his bride, Christine, and who, it was later charged, was flogged into signing a confession. A commission appointed by the Association for Criminal Justice investigated the charges and found that Colletti was not coerced into the confession.
>
> Cook said in the radio interview that it was not his intention to question the findings of the commission "so far as they went;" but, he expressed the opinion that the group could have gone farther [*sic*] and made a more serious study of the case.
>
> "I believe that the admission of Chief Matowitz that he had seen a piece of rubber hose around police headquarters, and further evidence that a piece of rubber hose is carried in all patrol wagons and squad cars is evidence that there is brutality used. If not, why the hose?"
>
> "In your opinion are third-degree methods justified to obtain evidence?" Levin asked Cook.

"Absolutely not. Justice cannot be achieved by crime or brutality."[49]

Police prosecutor Norman Ryan was on schedule to rebut Cook's arguments the following week.

Tony was just 18 when he was arrested on August 2, 1930, after his bride had been found murdered. After 26 hours of severe grilling and abuse he signed a confession. He was then given medical treatment by a police night nurse and a police doctor, and his injuries were also examined by a former prosecuting attorney and two deputy sheriffs. To all of these persons he complained of the beatings. His circumstantial written statement to his attorney describes almost continuous questioning, prolonged standing, deprivation of food and water, repeated striking, beating with what he thought was a rubber hose.... The police medical record reports "bruises left and right hips" and notes his complaints of beating. The former prosecutor also describes these bruises, which so impressed him that he showed them to the deputy sheriffs.

The case against Colletti rested on his confession, which he repudiated. Colletti's attorney (assigned by the court) became aroused at the treatment and planned to expose the practices at the trial, with five witnesses and the medical record to corroborate the boy. He made no secret of his intention, but he did not carry it out. On the day the trial was to open Colletti was found dead in his cell, hanging by a short belt to a pipe some distance over his head. His cell mates reported that he had committed suicide.[50]

In the Colletti case, a 1930 affair, the rubber hose or some weapon of similar type left marks, which were seen by an exceptional number of witnesses. An officer was in the adjoining room. One man of unusual intelligence and education, confined for a time in the Cleveland jail, declared a soft sandbag, sausage-shaped and bound in dark cloth, had been described to him by other prisoners, and that he had seen it. Two other torture devices appeared: in a certain murder case, one man declared he had been kept standing continuously for a thirty-hour period, another for thirty-six hours; both exhibited their feet, which were discolored and swollen, as proof. Colletti, too, declared he had been kept standing in a corner, over a period of many hours, being jolted or slapped whenever his knees sagged or he sought support by touching the wall. One of the murder suspects had exhibited discolored arms and shoulders, and stated that his arms had been twisted. The only corroboration possible in such cases is medical, and this, obviously, would be hard to obtain....[51]

For sure, one mourner inching forward to view the body had something painfully in common with Tony Colletti. Numbered with the humble, Joe brushed shoulders with the prominent. Politicians and judges, friend and foe alike, made their way to Cook's flower-blanketed casket for a final look at the aptly described "great mixer."

Popularly identified in politics as a Harry Davis Republican, Cook nonetheless had in his wide circle of friends men in public life who were affiliated with both major party organizations. His personal loyalty to friends transcended party lines.[52]

Many in the crowded living room had seen the towering black man with Cook at partisan rallies—Republican Cook had been known to make forceful speeches for Democrats as well.

"I know 213 reasons why you should re-elect Judge Mathias," Cook would say at Party of Lincoln gatherings (candidate Weygandt's name and a slightly different speech being substituted at the meetings of Democrats). The chief reason—equally [as] good for the elephant or the donkey—was one that was closest to Cook's own heart personally.

"And it should be for every person in the state who stands for a square deal for the underdog."

Cook would then point out that a square deal was not what the opposing party's candidate for judgeship stood for. He had only to remind his audience of the deal the man accompanying him that night had received.

"And Joe Weaver is here tonight."

With that, the audience would turn in their seats towards the entrance.

Every morning, bright and early, Joe, a novel part of the Cook Technique in political campaigning, would appear at Cook's office.

"You got the list of tonight's meetings made up yet, Mistuh Cook?"

Never did the grateful man fail to be exactly 45 minutes early to the meeting where he was scheduled so dramatically to appear.[53]

The annual handshake ritual had just taken place in 1932 when local newspapers made much ado of Nate Cook's sentence to jail and a 100-dollar fine and costs for contempt of court.

The high-spirited, unconventional lawyer and his associate, Emanuel M. Rose, had failed to appear before the Bench, and had not notified the court that a client of theirs had jumped bond. In passing sentence, the judge said that Cook, embarrassed by his client's act, had expressed displeasure to his partner in language "unfit to be repeated."[54]

The next date after sentence was imposed, Joe Weaver knocked at Cook's office. He said: "Mistuh Cook, suh. I ain't got any money for your defense fund, but I got a lot of time. I'll be glad to go in and serve every one of those five days for you."[55]

Joe Weaver was a man, said reporter Roelif Loveland in a feature article, and he was six feet four and he held ingratitude to be a grievous sin.[56]

Joseph Weaver, 1936 photo.

Photographer unlocated

CHAPTER 3

"UP SOUTH"

The train from Georgia carried the Weavers to their chosen Promised Land. They saw no demeaning signs when they stepped off the coach. No colored restroom signs in Cleveland. No colored waiting room. No water fountain from which the colored child should drink while wondering about the taste of white water. On the streetcar if they took seats in the rear, it was by choice, not because a posted sign pointed them there. As for housing and jobs, de facto discrimination certainly existed in the city, but both the Urban League and the NAACP were in place to aid in the fight against it.

The couple moved into the East Side enclave of 34,000 blacks. Their new hometown was a city vying for rank in the Midwest's cultural development, civic enthusiasm, and industrial growth. With its buckets of molten steel and synchronized pistons, Cleveland was emerging as an iron and steel magnet of labor from across the Atlantic as well as below the Mason Dixon. European arrivals were eager to work in the industrial centers of the Midwest. The urban North, unlike the South, had no Negro jobs begging for laborers. Foreign workers competed for the most menial work. At the same time, the steady movement of the black race out of the South augmented northerners' distrust and fear, and stirred resentment towards black competition.

Such sentiments fueled the argument that the Negro could earn a living more easily in the South than in the North, and a debate smoldered over which region was the better place for blacks to thrive. Joe Weaver had no reason to suspect in 1923 that his name was destined to become a part of that interregional controversy.

In the part of the country from which Weaver had departed, blacks who stayed in their place of inferiority often found a spirit of helpfulness. In the part to which he had come, urban dwellers were becoming increasingly concerned over the customs rural blacks brought with them to teeming sections of major cities. The caricatured sycophant of the 19th century South had turned into a repulsive stereotype that bred contempt in the 20th century North.

Whites were not alone in such resistance. Even among blacks, the South was increasingly heralded as the best place for the race to develop. Fear prevailed among many northern blacks that the southern Johnny-come-lately would bring with him his Jim Crow problems—and Jim Crow solutions.

In Cleveland, *Gazette* owner Harry Smith regularly featured the unbridled opinions of Reverend William A. Byrd in his weekly publication. Beneath provocative headlines such as: "Southernizing the North a Great Menace," Byrd took aim at the nation's running racial sores, varying only the target of his searing comments as he drew a bead on every racial problem in sight, North and South. The Jersey City minister even went so far as to say that the "Negro problem" was not exclusively the "white man's" problem to solve.

> The one great evil confronting this country is the attempt on the part of white and black southerners coming north to bring their southern traditions and customs and force them upon other people who hate them. Southern Negroes with their "jimcrow" [sic] beliefs and customs are unfitting the race to live in the north [sic]. The vilest prejudice and hatred imaginable these people bring with them and hold. Their hatred of a white face on the one hand, as well as their fear of a white face on the other, make the southern Negro, too often, a menacing problem in the north....[57]

Though discomfited by some of Byrd's hard edges, Editor Smith urged careful and thoughtful reading of the New Jerseyite's diatribe. Continuing his preachments, the minister wrote:

> [The North] should be counseled to have patience, while the unprepared Afro-American immigrant should be taught to prepare himself for northern civilization. Too often is the attempt being made to introduce into the North the policies and plans our people pursued in the South. The North is no place for them. We stand in great danger of having too large an ignorant population of our people in the North which is averse to becoming intelligent....
>
> The clinging to emotional fiascos and boisterous harangues by the majority of the colored people of this country is one of our saddest predicaments. Education, intelligent leadership, frugality, economy and polished manners we need greatly. The North, [illegible] will turn en mass [sic] against the colored race in their midst if we do not seek to show forth those finer qualities which we have mentioned....[58]
>
> It is now time for the race to learn that it must struggle years and years for education like other races. The premium the race puts upon ignorance must be speedily removed.... The ignorance, immorality, low state of civilization and semi-religious practices that colored people in the South have are due directly to the influence of southern whites.
>
> The greatest task before the American government today is to get the southern white man to be just toward the colored race.... However, we fear that the brutality of southern whites has so embittered the colored race in the South that it is practically unprepared to manifest the high principles of Christianity because of their resentment and bitterness toward the whites for the injustice forced upon them. Negroes owe to southern whites their meanness.
>
> The behavior of northern blacks is causing them to find themselves more and more unwelcome at hotels and restaurants in the North. The civilization of the North must not be ruined because of the willful and ignorant southerner, white or black.[59]

Reverend Byrd believed that biblical Christianity could have been the salvation of unlettered southern black worshipers had it been taught to them with the charity of its divine founder.

Sensitive though he was to attacks on his race by any perpetrator, Harry Smith underscored the strong views of the New Jersey Presbyterian preacher. To his readers the editor said: If more of our ministers had the gumption to lead their congregations instead of being led by them, it would be infinitely better for all concerned....[60]

One such local minister, Reverend Horace C. Bailey, led the flock at Antioch Baptist Church. Loaded with gumption, the Cleveland pastor's civic sermons, like those of Reverend Byrd, were a staple in the *Gazette*.

> I observe, having been in public life for forty years or more, that our great lack is education. Our pulpits need it; Sunday School teachers need it, as well as our laity in general....
>
> Let us not deceive ourselves into thinking that God is going to entrust us with the responsibility of leadership without preparation.... Our day to lead will come in proportion as we prepare ourselves intellectually and morally. We are just jokers and funmakers as yet. We study, it seems to me, to entertain—to amuse. We are too light-hearted. We laugh while the funeral pyre is around one of our group, and are not moved to sympathy and action by shrieks and groans. We give dances and parties while the political, civil and financial fires are burning around us. We are dumb to our position here in America with more than half of our group in political and civil slavery and our freedom in the North gradually slipping away from us. We have our heads ostrich-like under the sand, imagining we are safe. We must educate or perish.
>
> *No one can successfully enslave or impose upon an educated people.* [Italics added.]
>
> I am making this appeal to our young men and women who are making it hard for themselves and the race. Too much foolishness, too much loafing, too much boisterousness on our streets. There is no excuse for any young woman or man to be

ignorant now for the education facilities are too numerous. Ignorance is a crime nowadays.

I plead with you to cease your follies and let us all get down to race-building. Let the higher up of the race cease card-playing and parlor-dancing and get on with race-building. You nor I cannot rise above our body politic. We must lift up this mass [*sic*] or go down with them....

Our preachers must and should urge upon our group the great necessity for education for this generation if we are to cope with the other races in our country.[61] [Italics added.]

Even among blacks, the South was increasingly heralded as the best place for the race to develop. The wide disparity of educational opportunities in the southern states had left many of them ill-equipped to compete in the labor markets of northern cities, and, in the opinion of some observers like Reverend W. H. Hudnut, unfit even to live in an urban environment. Though a northern resident and black, Hudnut stood with southern proponents who believed that Negroes in almost every respect were not as well off in the North as they were in the South.

"The southern folk understand him (the Negro) better. Climatic conditions in the South favor him (the Negro) and the colored men who come North from the South are not familiar with the mode of living here in the manufacturing centers to which they have been sent. They are not fitted for this new life," said the Cleveland minister, in a speech at old Rayen Campus in the Youngstown area.[62]

Irked though he was by the Reverend's lambasting comments, Harry Smith nonetheless fairly gave them voice, but editorially disagreed.

Reverend W. H. Hudnut's statement... shows that he is not at all familiar with conditions he sought to discuss. More than a half million Negroes have come to the North in the last five or six years and fully 95 percent of them have remained and are here to stay....

> If the relations between the races in this section of the country are not satisfactory (and they are), the relations between the races in the South are infinitely worse in every respect. Indeed, this latter explains perfectly the southern Negroes' emigration to the North in recent years. Whatever the Negro immigrant is, today, he is undoubtedly what mistreatment in the South has made him....[63]

They (blacks) ought to stay in the South, whites above the Mason-Dixon believed, with many African Americans in agreement. White urban workers said *they* ought to stay in the country, at the same time that white farmers in the Midwest insisted *they* should not be allowed to compete with them for land.

The "southernizing" of the North was indeed widely dreaded.

Into such a racial climate Joe and Orrie Weaver arrived in the spring of 1923, and planted their seeds of expectation in supposedly fertile soil. Orrie worked as a domestic in their new hometown. Joe found work at a steel plant for six months, doing odd jobs. In the fall, he was assigned steady work on the loading dock. Teamed with an old friend from Georgia, he spray-painted Ford frames.

The process was simple. An overhead crane delivered a stack of frames to the work station for painting. The team placed a frame onto a workbench, sprayed it, and then stacked the painted frame on a low, flatbed truck. One of the men pushed the truck to a location where a crane loaded stacks of frames onto a railroad car for shipment. But when the overhead crane was operating elsewhere, Joe—like a Samson—acted as his own crane. His pay was earned on a piecework basis.

Six days a week Joe worked at Midland Steel. As time went by, he thought about doing another kind of work. According to the tabloid circulating in his community in 1923, 20,000 Afro-Americans were currently employed in the postal department. Fifteen thousand were carriers, 3,000 post-office clerks, 2,000 railway postal clerks and about 700 laborers. Joe envisioned himself carrying mail while wearing the prestigious uniform of a United States postal worker.[64]

The postal service code required a mail carrier to be honest, sober, loyal, and industrious, as well as neat and circumspect in his attire, a man of integrity and responsibility, meeting all his financial obligations promptly. He had to live decently, and... always present a neat personal appearance....

Having met these requirements, the applicant for the position of letter carrier or post office clerk must pass an open competitive examination conducted by the Civil Service Commission with an average percentage of not less than 70.[65]

None of these specifications troubled Joe except for the written exam, schooled as he was to grade six in the rural South. To raise his chances of passing the test, he enrolled in night school in 1924 as he had done in Atlanta two years earlier.

Cleveland had taken on an issue fermenting after the turn of the century: the steady arrival of illiterate descendants of slaves from a part of the country that feared the economic and social consequences of educating them. The African-American population, just 1.5 percent in Cleveland in 1910, had ballooned by 308 percent, its white population by 38 percent. (Still, the white population of more than 762,000 was at 96 percent; the black was just under four percent.) The city had a program in effect for adult coloreds, in 1923 winning commendation for its efforts to meet the challenge of integrating an illiterate people that had little in common with the industrial North.

Adult night schools were everywhere. In 1903, Cleveland led the nation when it established schools that aided the foreign-born in passing their naturalization exams.[66]

Throughout the city, the board of education had pressed into service public schools and libraries, settlement houses, factories, and even hospitals and homes. The Citizen's Bureau helped the foreign-born residents of Cuyahoga County to Americanize in culture as well as in law. Candidates were taught English and the essentials of America's history, its government, and other institutions. Twice a year, in February and July, graduation exercises of citizenship classes were held.[67]

Cleveland had a fermenting problem regarding illiterate Americans and faced up to the situation with several special classes for the adult colored.

Joe Weaver took advantage of the program set up for the colored migrants. His diligence in studying English and Citizenship (Americanization) at R. B. Hayes evening school rivaled the efforts of the foreign-born adult student. Such effort, coupled with exemplary deportment, won the praise of his teacher, the wife of a Methodist minister.

When he was not spray-painting at Midland, singing in the choir at Zion Hill, or learning from his teacher at R. B. Hayes, Joe took orders for men's suits. He carried around a suitcase with samples of the company's fabrics and sent orders to Atlas Tailoring in Chicago.

Within four years of his arrival in Cleveland, Joe had in place a solid foursquare foundation of home, job, church, and school.

Then came 1927. A momentous year in the nation's history. Americans and the world applauded Charles Lindbergh's nonstop flight from New York to Paris in 33.5 hours, and marveled at Al Jolson's voice in *The Jazz Singer*, the first talkie. That year Kern's and Hammerstein's *Show Boat* became the talk of New York City.

In that year also, Drinker and Shaw developed the iron lung, and the Holland Tunnel opened as the first vehicular tunnel linking New York and New Jersey. Abe Saperstein organized the Harlem Globetrotters black basketball team and Babe Ruth hit 60 home runs for the New York Yankees. The fashionable danced the fox-trot while Johnny Weissmuller swam 100 yards in 51 seconds. Alabama tied Stanford in the Rose Bowl and New York defeated Pittsburgh four straight in the World Series.

Out West, the deepest well in the world went down 8,000 feet in Orange County. Back East, the fifteen-millionth Model T Ford came off the line. It was also a year that sheared the nation's emotions: national angst over the execution of Nicola Sacco and Bartolomeo Vanzetti, immigrants charged with murder in 1920.

Even if all those milestones had faded from the nation's memory, for dreadful reasons of his own, 1927 would remain a year Joe Weaver would never forget. In February, his wife Orrie left him, so he moved into a rooming house. On Saturday, March 5, he quit his job at the steel plant and found another job the following Monday morning. He started working the same day at Hydraulic Steel.

Eight days later, his foursquare foundation collapsed like a sinkhole and he dropped through to a hell on earth.

It happened to the Georgia-born ex-sharecropper in Cuyahoga County, Ohio.

It happened to Joe Weaver "up South."

CHAPTER 4

MIDLAND STEEL

Sunday, March 13, 1927, was a wet and unseasonably warm day in the north coast city. Rain clouds hovered over a far West Side neighborhood, the hub of which was a booming steel plant begun as the Parish and Bingham Company. In its earliest years after 1894, it fashioned metal into curry combs, sprockets, bicycles, and Ingersoll dollar watch cases. In 1908, it took on the fabrication of all frames for Ford Model T and a substantial portion of Model A frames. A few years later, it tooled up to produce army trucks and bombs for the Army-Air Force. By 1923, under a new name, it supplied the transportation industry with steel frames, axle housings, and heavy steel stampings for automobiles, trucks, and buses.

Midland Steel was a nonunion shop, a place where fathers encouraged sons to follow in their footsteps. It was a place where a man who could hit a fast-pitched softball on the company ball diamond or play a musical instrument in the company band was assured a job—all while earning a good living.

Inside the steel plant, working with speed and accuracy along assembly lines, second shift employees drummed out their share of the 10,000 Ford frames the plant generated daily in that banner year. Outside the plant in the damp and dark, the company guard was making his rounds.

Until three months before when several of his fingers were sliced off by a machine, 28-year-old Jasper Riley Russell had worked inside the plant. The raven-haired, blue-eyed Jasper was the fifth of eight siblings. Seeking work, he had come to northeastern Ohio from Irondale, a small town on the Ohio River near the West Virginia border. Two of his older brothers had already left northern Jefferson County looking elsewhere for jobs. Another two had died, one in 1924 at age 24, the other at six months of age. Jasper's father had dutifully carried the coffin of the infant son on his shoulder five miles to the cemetery.

Sherman Russell was a devoted husband and father. Before working as a kiln fireman at a local brickyard, he had been a horse-and-buggy mail carrier. He provided for a family and two horses on $85 per month, pulling ends together by the bartering he did along his mail route. Customers gave him meat, poultry, and vegetables. In return, he brought them small items from town. Still, Sherman used to quip to his youngsters around the dinner table, "when there's butter on the bread, there's no jelly. When there's jelly, no butter."

All of the Russells were of slight build. Mary Higgins Russell, though frail and sickly most of her life, was undiminished in her Christian faith. Much of her time was spent in prayer at home, in church, and in prayer meetings in neighbors' homes, her pious footsteps a path for her children to follow. Jasper's walk therein led him to preaching in the Methodist church, and ministering to the needs of others around Irondale. But with his brothers gone, his acts of charity began at home with his aging mother.

The year after his discharge from the Army, Jasper left for Cleveland. He moved into a boarding house on Madison Avenue not far from where he worked. Soon he enrolled in Bible college with an eye on the cleric's collar.

On the evening of March 13, 1927, however, the mild-mannered young man was in uniform on patrol, a watchman's cap on his dark hair. What was not on his 5-foot, 4-inch frame was a watchman's firearm. After all, nothing bad had ever happened at Midland—Jasper's words to his brother William who once visited him at the plant. Besides, Jasper had said, anybody out to get him would probably catch him by surprise and shoot him from behind.

Jasper strolled down a cinder path towards the call box in the carpenters' shop. He passed by a wood shed that once was the watchman's shanty.

Suddenly, like a dart afire, a bullet cracked the darkness and pierced the night guard's head, coming to rest in his eye socket. It dropped him to the ground. Thick, warm blood oozed from his minced right eye, soaking the earth under his jaw.

Moments after 11:00 p.m., the automatic warning sounded at American District Telegraph. Thomas Dever, an ADT roundsman, took off for the plant.

A half hour later he was met by Jesse Schwab. The plant foreman knew the location of all the watchman's call boxes. Schwab and Dever followed the watchman's line of clocks and hurried over to the carpenters' shop. Not finding Jasper there, they hustled down the cinder path past the wood shanty towards the main office building. A hundred feet or so from the carpenters' shop, they came upon a body lying prostrate on the ground.

The next morning, Cleveland detectives made the rounds of the day shift workers. They hoped someone had overheard talk of a robbery. No one had, but the detectives discovered tools scattered about the floor of the cashier's office. Nearby was a damaged safe. A window in the office had been broken, the lock on it forced. Outside the window was a short ladder. When the investigators learned where the tools were normally kept, they concluded that the break-in had been done by someone familiar with the layout of the plant.

There were two burglars and they were amateurs, the press was told. Detective Lieutenant Frank Story said his men had found two sets of footprints outside the window and two rifled billfolds a short distance from where the body had been found. The empty billfolds were assumed to belong to the victim.

"Possibly it was someone who knew the plant. They tried to get in the one window that was directly above the safe. Then they picked up tools that we identify as coming from the plant— a hack saw, a screw driver, and other small things real cracksmen wouldn't carry. They were tedious and almost useless for opening a small safe like this."

The main safe in another room was untouched. The safe which was attacked was a much smaller strongbox used for accessory storing purposes.

Instead of an explosive having been used to blow off the doors of the safe, as professionals would do, the marauders tried to unfasten the bolts that hold them, and a bent screw driver was found jammed into one bolt crevice.

"Russell must have chased one of them outdoors, and then probably the other man shot him from behind."

The watchman had no gun on him, and a weapon believed to have been his was found in Russell's locker.[68]

In a search of the grounds, homicide detectives noticed that two strands of barbed wire, supported by an iron rod, had pulled away from the fence. One of the men reached up on the wire and picked off a small piece of brown cloth that looked like overcoat material. They took their finding to the superintendent's office and talked with company officials, hoping for the name of someone who owned a coat of matching material. The names of several colored men who had not shown up for work that day were offered.

Bertillon experts took photographs of fingerprints on the safe and the window. Meanwhile, the neighborhood was canvassed. An employee of a gas station on the next corner from the plant told the policemen he had been on duty the night of the murder. He had heard a noise around 10:40 p.m., he said, either a gunshot or a car backfiring, but he wasn't sure. He saw an auto "draw up" to the plant about that time.

Twenty-year-old Kitty Stevens lived across the street from Midland. She told the detectives at her door that two men in a Ford coupe had driven back and forth in front of her house the day before the murder, eyeing the plant. Armed with that bit of information, the police investigators returned to the plant and checked the employment lists for the owner of an automobile of the kind Kitty had described.

> Three suspects were arrested early Monday and...held at Central Station.
>
> Detective Inspector Cody declared he was confident police knew the identity of the slayers. The suspects were picked up when police learned they were disgruntled when discharged from the division plant recently when they objected to a cut in pay.[69]

At 1:00 in the morning, Detective Lieutenant Frank Story announced to the press that a confession to the slaying of Jasper Russell was "expected momentarily."

> A piece of cloth torn from an overcoat was found in the bushes near the scene yesterday. Blood was also discovered on the briers. An employee, who worked Saturday but failed to appear yesterday, was arrested at his home late in the day. The piece of cloth matched his overcoat, which had been recently patched, and his hands bore fresh scratches, detectives said.
>
> He had been grilled continuously for eight hours, and was taken to the scene, but declared he was innocent. Several discrepancies, according to police, appeared in the stories told by the man and his wife.
>
> Detectives are confident that he was one of the two or three who were caught by Russell while cracking the safe in the cashier's office.
>
> The man said he did not go to work yesterday because of a pain in his chest. His wife said when she called him, he was suffering from stomach trouble.
>
> Three others, all recently employed in the plant...were being held.
>
> Detective Inspector Cornelius W. Cody, who thinks the murder will be cleared up at once, said he believed the men in custody included participants in the unsuccessful attempt to break into

the safe, and probably the man who shot Russell in the head as he was making his trip of inspections.

Cody was surer than ever last night that the crime was the work of men who knew the "inside layout" of the plant.

Two of the men held and the two being hunted had previously been discharged from the Midland Steel Products Co.

E. J. Kulas, president of the Midland Steel Company...posted a $1,000 reward for information leading to the arrest and conviction of the killers.

"A few months ago, Russell lost two fingers in an accident at the plant. He was a wonderful, well-liked chap, so rather than retire him, we thought we'd give him the watchman's job," said the portly, balding company president, a jovial man when all was well at Midland.

Kulas also believed that the men who cracked the safe and killed Russell knew the lay of the ground and were probably connected with the plant at one time or another.[70]

At 1:30 in the morning, a fresh pair of interrogators took over.

[They] questioned [Alex] Mayner incessantly thruout [*sic*] Monday night, and the early hours of Tuesday morning saw him crumple before the inquisitorial fire and admit his part in the robbery. In a signed confession Mayner told of the events that led to the shooting.[71]

Alex Mayner named his Sunday evening accomplice. [The accomplice's name was not published in the following article.]

Mayner prefaced his story of the conspiracy with a statement his wages had been reduced.

"_____ and I framed the plot to go to the company early Monday and break into the safe. He took a gun. While bending over the safe we heard the watchman approaching thru the corridor. We made for a window, got out and ran down a cinder path. I hid in a carpenter shop, and_____ placed himself behind a shed.

"The watchman was still unaware of us, and kept on ringing his boxes. He came down the cinder path we had taken, and prepared to ring the box at the shed where_____ was hiding.

"_____ saw the watchman and knew that he was discovered and was recognized. He shot once—and the watchman fell with a bullet hole in the back of his head."[72]

On March 15, 1927, while Jasper Russell's body lay in the morgue, political analyst Louis B. Seltzer proffered in a headline a question for readers of the *Press* to ponder.

What Price Life?

If life is ever held by man to be more precious and full of praise than at any other time of his existence, it is as he approaches 30.

It makes not much difference, so far as life is concerned, whether the man of almost 30 is a night watchman for a factory or the owner of the factory itself—life is just as precious for him and as full of promise, whatever he may be.

Jasper Russell was 28. He was a night watchman at the Parrish & Bingham division of Midland Steel Company on West 106th Street.

For Jasper Russell, as for other young men of his years, the novelty of running a steel blade over his face to shear off the stubbles of young manhood had worn off somewhat. He had become used to slipping into long trousers. He had gained poise and confidence in himself.

Maturity of perspective had replaced adolescent instability. He faced life as life—with all of its problems. Its real significance had not many years before broken through the clouds of uncertain wonderment, bright, clear and shining. He had, as other young men, looked forward to the time when he was to be what he was at his age—a full grown man. Life in all of its richness extended before him.

Jasper Russell made the rounds of the plant Sunday night as usual. They found his body early Monday in the mill yard of the plant with a bullet through the head. Safe robbers had cut him down.

Every reader is shocked with the horror of the incident. The cutting down of this young man in the full bloom of life strikes out at them in all of its gruesome details.

But in the reading of the story of Jasper Russell's death we couldn't help but think of the other things that have cut down men of Jasper Russell's age. War, for instance. Unnecessary war. War of intolerance. Wars promoted and executed by men for dollars—life regardless.

Jasper Russell at 28 was unmarried. Not all men at 28 are unmarried. Most of them have their homes. Large homes or small homes. Owned by them or rented. But "their homes," nevertheless.

Let's grant that the last military holocaust was fought for the peace of the world. For the protection of the rest of the world against the economic aggressions of one nation. Millions of men— a vast majority of them Jasper Russell's age, or a little younger, or a little older—live in the memories of this and other countries through small white crosses near the battlefields where they lost their lives. Hundreds of thousands of others bear living witness to the fact that they also were willing to give their lives.

We all want to see the flag protected. We all want to see the lives and property of American citizens, wherever they may be, in Nicaragua, or in Mexico, in China or in Africa, protected by the flag. But we don't want, any of us, to interfere with the rights of other people. We don't want to have a small group of men in places of power, political or economic, do things that make it necessary for us to be plunged into a war whose purpose is doubtful.

We are willing to sacrifice our lives when it will do the world some good. Protect those weaker than ourselves. Make the world a better place in which to live—if the rattle of muskets and the spread of poison gas achieves [sic] such an end. It isn't a question of reckless courage. It isn't a question of cowardice. It's a question of sanity and tolerance.

There isn't much difference, after all is said and done, in cutting men down in the full bloom of life on the battlefields of an unnecessary war, or in the heat of intolerance, than in safe robbers sending a bullet through the head of Jasper Russell.

Yet there is one difference. Instead of one Jasper Russell sacrificing his life, millions do.

Early the next day, March 15th, Cleveland detectives showed up at the Hydraulic Steel Company seeking a named employee on the job barely one week. Coming upon him from behind, they slapped handcuffs on the startled man.

Joe Weaver found himself under arrest for murder. Bound for jail in the Promised Land of his choosing.

CHAPTER 5

SWEATING

On the way to the police station, the arresting officers stopped by East 57th Street for a search of their suspect's room in his presence. The next day policemen returned to the rooming house and took Joe's landlady and her niece into custody.[73]

That same day the president of Midland Steel paid a visit to the police station on Champlain Street. He wanted to personally congratulate Detective Chief Cornelius Cody.

"I'm mighty proud of the Cleveland police department, its detectives and their head for their excellent work in clearing up this brutal murder," Kulas told Cody.

"Scarcely two days have passed since Russell's body was found in the mill yard, and now you have the alleged murderer in custody," he continued.

"Such work speaks highly for the efficiency of the Cleveland police department and the ability of its executives and detectives. Few police departments of the country could have solved a crime so rapidly," he asserted.

Cody smiled pleasantly.

"We appreciate being appreciated," was his reply.[74]

The chief told news reporters he expected his men would have a confession that day.

> While Kulas was praising Cody and the police department, a tall, young colored man was being questioned in a room nearby. Detectives pressed him with a constant fire of questions regarding the brutal murder, ...but he stubbornly denied any knowledge of the crime.[75]

The names of people he said could confirm his whereabouts after 10:00 the evening of the murder spurted from Joe Weaver's mouth. Grilling continued throughout night. Around daybreak a diminutive man of 43 was brought into the room by a fourth detective.

> "Why don't you tell the truth?" the suspect shouted into the face of the man he had accused of slaying Jasper Russell. "You know you were there!"
>
> "You're a [expletive deleted] liar," the suspect shouted and lunged at Mayner.
>
> Before detectives could pull them apart, Mayner was held tightly by the larger adversary who [the questioners said] was attempting to bite him.[76]

The interrogators pressed on with a constant fire of questions, to which their suspect said:

> He was at home at the time of the murder; he looked at his watch as he entered the door; he knows he could have been nowhere else....[77]

According to the detectives, the interrogated man had gone to Mayner's house to obtain a gun he had loaned some time ago, but left the house without securing it. Told the gun was still at Mayner's house, the detectives searched the place but could not find it. They also found no one in the house who had seen the gun being examined by the two men, as the accusing suspect said.

The reputed "triggerman" denies he holds any animosity against the company for discharging him a week ago and claims that Mayner's charge is a "frame-up."[78]

Elsewhere in the station, another link was forged through a woman in custody. She told the detectives that she had given the accused man a revolver. After she gave him the gun, he and his accomplice, she said, went to the steel plant that Sunday night to rob the company's safe.[79]

Newsmen milled about the police station on the third day of interrogation. They were anxious for confirmation of the promised confession only to be told that the department was certain the killer was in custody, and that it intended to recommend the reward go to Kitty Stevens who lived across the street from the plant.

Four days after the murder, the *Cleveland Press* ran a curious story with an arresting headline:

Quails Under 30-Hour Prayer
Killer Suspect Facing Novel Third Degree

Continuous moaning of prayer droned into its 30th hour Thursday noon in a cell at Central Police Station. In the next cell another man had tried all night not to listen. At noon he crumpled and broke into tears, half-mad at the supplicating voices.

Alex Mayner, confessed member of the safecracking gang that murdered Jasper Russell, night watchman at the Parish and Bingham plant of the Midland Steel Co., was begging divine forgiveness.

The unwilling listener had been named by Mayner as the trigger man in the murder. He had denied all connection with the crime.

Mayner started his prayer Wednesday morning. Wednesday night his wife, Viola, joined him. Together the two kneeled on the stone floor. All night long their voices pleaded. The other man cowered in the dark. The voices became saws on his taut nerves.

He begged them to stop. Put his fingers in his ears, grew frantic, and broke into helpless tears.

Relentlessly the voices implored.

Detectives expected the listener to "break" Thursday afternoon.[80]

The third degree stretched over three days. Novel or otherwise administered, Joe Weaver did not break.

CHAPTER 6

THE "HOLE" ON THE SQUARE

Six days after the arrest, the county grand jury indicted the steel worker for first-degree murder. Two days later, he stood in arraignment, a foot taller than the man standing next to him. Judge Walter McMahon said the two of them would be tried separately, Joe Weaver on April 11th; Alex Mayner a week later.

Each man pled not guilty and asked for legal representation. Later, Judge Irving J. Carpenter from Norwalk appointed each man's counsel. Following the arraignment, the sheriff took both men into custody to await trial in County Jail.

Labeled the "Black Hole of Cuyahoga County," the jail was a medieval stone bastille tucked away in a cranny off the northwest corner of Public Square. Just three years before Joe Weaver arrived there, it ranked third among the filthiest, most wretched lockups in the nation. That was the consensus of a committee on tour of the nation's jails and penitentiaries. For years, grand juries had inspected the grotesque incubator of crime and breeding place for disease, and had made their findings known to the court in reports that varied little.

Until his fate was decided, the former sharecropper would spend his out-of-court time in the facility built in 1875 when the county's population was about 155,000. Except for the

57

courthouse, the jail was the only building from that era still standing on the Square. If occupancy was at its normal daily number of 300, Joe was moved into a cell with another person or two. Peaks of 400 to 480 inmates at a time were not unheard of in the place designed for 136 persons.

Scores of human beings—the innocent and the guilty, the sane and the insane, the sick and the well, the quick and the dying, the traffic violator and the murderer, the witness and the criminal, the young and the old, the first offender and the hardened criminal—all were submerged in a common swamp of disease, filth, and moral degradation. Entering the jail, Joe Weaver was subjected to the injurious gases and the strong odor of disinfectants, the constant use of which was made necessary by the out-of-date and inadequate plumbing facilities.... In the various quarters of the jail, lungs of occupants burned from injurious gases; nasal passages suffered irritation from strong disinfectants that futilely masked foul odors. High up the wall of his eight by ten cell a small begrimed window, barred and securely fastened, blocked outside air of relief. A stark light bulb suspended in the center of the cell dispensed gloom. Against the wall, an old and corroded toilet passed but a portion of feces disintegrated in urine, slime, and vomit to a basement cesspool, then belched up the stench from it. Untrapped toilets in the cells flushed periodically in unison. Pillows and newspapers stuffed by inhabitants into uncovered commodes proved futile. Germs wafted through the dimly lit cells and dark corridors, conveyed by an antiquated ventilating system to the kitchen in the basement where prowling cats kept sentry for their reportedly three-month life span. The scavengers made their rounds among broken sewer pipes in the engine rooms, creeping from the jail kitchen to the pantry. Back and forth to garbage cans until disease and death stopped their sordid meandering.

Vermin crept, crawled, and scurried across the kitchen floor. Disinfectants and eradicators only worsened the air. Sore throats were common. Tonsillitis, and in some cases diphtheria, were diagnosed. Venereal disease spread unencumbered. Healthy arrivals found themselves exposed to contagious and infectious diseases as they ate and slept with strangers, every act of privacy in the view of others.[81]

Joe's aged mother and his sister Susie had just ended their visit to the dungeon when the latticed steel door of countless rivets opened up and two men stepped into the cell. The stocky, slightly red-haired one clenched his trademark cigar between his teeth. The other one, tall, winsome and graying, said, "My name is Bill Marsteller and this is Nate Cook."

The deep-voiced introduction was tinted with the drawl of a Kentuckian from Nicholasville. "We have been appointed by the court to defend you."

> Forty-one-year-old William Fish Marsteller had earned a law degree at the University of Michigan and had received his doctor of laws degree at the University of Geneva in Switzerland. Admitted to the Michigan and Ohio bars in 1918 and to the Kentucky bar in 1924, he [had] joined the faculty of the [Cleveland Marshall] law school in 1919.[82]

The give-and-take of a courtroom battle, the professor's passion, trumped lecturing in a schoolroom. There was a spring in his step whenever Marsteller had a case on his court calendar.

He and his partner listened as the indicted killer of Jasper Russell explained why he had quit Midland Steel.

> "And how did that paper with your name and address on it get in Mayner's pocket?" Nate Cook asked.
>
> "Well, Mr. Cook, I sold men's suits in my spare time, and Alex had just bought one from me. His wife liked it and she wanted me to get her some of the material. I went to Alex's house and told him I'd try to get it. I had moved, so I wrote my name and address on a sheet of paper and gave it to him."
>
> "And can you account for your movements the night of the murder?" asked Marsteller.
>
> "Yes, suh. My landlady will tell you that I didn't even leave the house that night."

"Well, Joe," said Nate Cook, "it's your word against Mayner's. I'm afraid it's going to be a long, hard fight."

Cook explained that the police had damaging statements, two from streetcar employees and another that they said came from Joe's landlady's niece.

"She won't be allowed to testify in court, but what she said probably will find its way into the prosecutor's case," Cook warned.[83]

The niece was five years old.

Cleft-chinned Edward Cornelius Stanton, at 38, was the county prosecutor. In November, 1926, the popular father of three had won an unprecedented fourth term. Voters, it was suggested in news editorials, could show their appreciation for their good fortune by re-electing the "people's prosecutor."

Smiling, affable, obliging, humorous, but he can be fiery on occasion was how the *Cleveland News* described the hard-nosed prosecutor. Support for him was so enthusiastic that the *News* editor equated a vote for Stanton to a vote against crime.

Tuesday's election gives the men and women of Cuyahoga county a pleasant opportunity to show that they appreciate good fortune when they have it. The good fortune is the chance to assure the community the services of Edward C. Stanton, truly the "people's prosecutor," as prosecuting attorney for two years more. As a moment's reflection will show, the opportunity is rare as well as valuable and should be seized without fail.

First elected to the office six years ago, Mr. Stanton made good emphatically from the beginning. That entitled him to a second term, under the rule that good work deserves recognition. The voters re-elected him with enthusiasm and the work of the prosecutor's office proved even better than before, since the two years of diligent and efficient service had a helpful aftereffect, as in leaving court dockets cleared of hang-over cases.

Two years ago, then, after two terms of conspicuous success as prosecuting attorney, Mr. Stanton could properly have asked election to the bench or to Congress, or to any office attracting his ambition, and the voters would have had every reason to consent. Instead, he was persuaded that the county still needed him on the old job, crime not being wholly extinct. So he asked, received and served a third term, with the usual perfect satisfaction to the public.

This year, with his accumulated renown for successful public service, Mr. Stanton might well have claimed promotion and the community might well have provided it. That he is willing to serve again in the important office he has made so useful is rare good luck, almost justifying a hope that he may be retained indefinitely for the public good as judges are.

Rightly called one of the best prosecuting attorneys the county ever had, Mr. Stanton is more of a force for good than some may realize, unless their memories are long. From the first he won the hearty admiration of *The News*, as of all good citizens by his zeal and success in sending murderers to the electric chair, breaking up robber gangs and making criminal law protect honest people. To him more than to any other is due the happy fact that Cleveland is no Chicago, no happy hunting ground for gunmen and thugs.... For being relatively free from notorious and unafraid [of] crime, Cleveland can thank Edward C. Stanton.

His office has many other duties than prosecuting criminals, of course, and all are performed splendidly. His notable record has commanded the approval of newspapers, organizations and citizens, regardless of party. All that can be said against him in campaign items is that he has offended certain special groups by insisting on being prosecutor for all the people, or that somebody else would like his job. We earnestly urge his re-election by an even bigger majority than usual, and as many future re-elections as he will accept....[84]

The win of approval came by a plurality of the votes.

Asked by a reporter back in 1922 what he thought was the reason he ran ahead of the tickets, Stanton had replied, "A realization on the part of the public that I am conscientious in my work and prosecute without fear or favor."

Pressure came with the job, Stanton said, at times very strong and hard to ignore. Such as when a mother comes in carrying a young baby in her arms, two or three other children trailing along, "and she makes a plea for her husband who should be sent to jail for the protection of society."

That clawed at the prosecutor.

"They will be left to battle with the world. Crime is always toughest on the innocent and helpless."

The reporter moved on to the matter of capital punishment by electrocution.

"I certainly do not [abhor it] when it is a deterrent to crime, but I'm satisfied in most cases when a jury brings in a recommendation for mercy, because I know the weight on their minds and consciences."

"What is the reason nobody has been indicted in the Hall-Mills murder case in New Brunswick, New Jersey?"

"The prosecutor there has no backbone," said Stanton.

Was money talking?

"Money can cover an investigation and place impediments in the paths of authorities unless immediate action is taken."

"Delay is bad for prosecution?"

"It makes it harder to get evidence…."

What would he have done had he been the prosecutor in New Brunswick? Cuyahoga county's prosecutor since 1921 was asked.

"The principal would have been indicted and placed on trial before this. That murder took place some eight or nine weeks ago. I would have bent every effort to make the guilty ones suffer the full extent of the law, whatever it is in New Jersey."

"Do you think the prosecutor there has talked too much?"

"He has made the mistake of promising the public some sensation for 'tomorrow.' He should have acted and not been scared out. He is there to prosecute and not to pamper."

Asked how he squared his professional ferociousness with the religion he had been taught by Father Haggeney at St. Ignatius, Stanton, known in his Irish neighborhood as the Wonder of Ward Eight, replied:

"The Bible also says an eye for an eye."

"Can you always tell if people are lying to you?"

"Not at first. If I am in doubt I just let them talk on and they convict themselves by their own words before they get through."

The prosecutor was asked where he wanted to go in the future.

"No place until I am ready for it. I always want to stay in the law business."

"Do you think there should be a public defender?" the newsman asked.

"No. The criminal would always have it in his mind that there would be someone ready to fight for his interest and that is against public morals. Criminals are shrewd enough without being helped; they often fool the cleverest lawyers."

"How about women? Do they make good jurors in murder cases?" the reporter asked.

"Yes, on the whole, but the younger ones do not appreciate the gravity of the situation. Those who are past twenty-five are all right and sensible. Those younger than twenty-five are invariably against the state and society, they favor the criminals. There are exceptions, of course, but as a rule 'society' means nothing to them. Maybe it is because their minds are immature....

"They are more straightforward. They do not try to wriggle out of serving on a trial. They are more attentive to testimony. But, of course, women are not infallible. Take a trial against a woman. Women are pretty unmerciful against their sisters. Men are more willing to recommend mercy. On the other hand, men have the same failing in a trial of a man. That is why, in first-degree cases, we try to select six men and six women.

"Six men and six women are safer for justice," the experienced prosecutor said.

"Sometimes women are capricious. It's a little difficult to find the reason for this."

Stanton suspected that women are prone to sentimentality. "... In most cases, women jurors recommend mercy, although the number opposed to capital punishment is no greater than among men when they are asked to serve on a jury.

"Housewives make desirable jurors. Young 'intellectuals' and college students don't. They are too advanced for common sense, yet their influence is strong...."

His ambition?

"To make Cleveland clean and having less crime than other cities of its size."

Stanton said further that he was supported by the mayor and had excellent help from the police department.

What did he think Cleveland needed?

"An organization of some kind to help men and women when they are released from prison and reformatory. They have nothing. The police are likely to hound them and they have slight incentive to go straight. Do you remember the Bishop in 'Les Miserables?' I always like to read about Jean Valjean and the Count of Monte Cristo."

What did he like doing best for recreation?

"Playing baseball with my boys and romping with my little girl."

Finally, the prosecutor was asked which he would rather do: ask questions or answer them. "Ask," replied Stanton. "It's easier."[85]

On April 11, 1927, the formidable prosecutor arrived at the courthouse. He was flanked by his young and able assistant of three years, James Charles Connell, who had joined the county prosecutor's office in 1924 after several years as a city police prosecutor. Golden-tongued courtroom orators of his day—none more persuasive than Ohio-born Clarence Darrow—had drawn him to the legal profession like a moth to a flame. The native Clevelander could have distinguished himself as a court reporter, having been a nimble-fingered shorthand expert who at age 18 had typed 108 words per minute to tie the professional record of showman Billy Rose. Connell, the son of a firefighter, chose instead to work at extinguishing the hope that flamed in the breasts of defendants.

The tug-of-war was about to begin. The hard-nosed prosecutor and his quiet-voiced but tough assistant on one side. A pair of adamant veteran defense attorneys on the other. On the line was the life of a black man. One some believed better off had he never left Georgia.

CHAPTER 7

CONVICTED IN CUYAHOGA COUNTY

The trial began on April 11, 1927. The first day was taken up with jury selection.

"You shall well and truly try, and true deliverance make, between the State of Ohio, and the prisoner of the bar, Joseph Weaver, so help you God."

So swore the selected jury of eleven men and two women on the second morning of the trial. The presiding judge decided that it would be fitting for the jury to have a view of the place where the murder had occurred. The next day the all-white panel and the Defendant were taken by the sheriff to Midland Steel.

Meanwhile, a tall dark-skinned woman was employing her tactics right outside the courthouse. She was a long way from her usual haunts, the street corners of Atlanta and Decatur. She had come to Cleveland to support her brother. The stropping, self-styled evangelist converted the courthouse steps into her praying ground. Every day of the trial, after strutting with the confidence of a peacock and armed with a rousing tambourine, Susie Weaver Smith got down on her knees before going inside. She was determined to "pray the locks off the jailhouse door!"

Proceedings began on the morning of the fourth day. The team from the prosecutor's office entered the courtroom, James

Connell to present the state's case. The Defendant entered next, brought in by the deputy sheriff, behind him his defense team. Thirteen law-abiding, registered voters of Cuyahoga filed into the jury stand. Ten of the jurors were white men, as was the alternate. On command, the gallery rose to its feet with the entry of Judge Irving Carpenter of Norwalk.

After opening statements, the state called its first witness, Thomas Dever. As an ADT roundsman, it was his duty to investigate the delinquencies of watchmen. Dever said the last ring from Midland Steel was at 10:30 p.m. From his statement, the state fixed the time of the murder at sometime between 10:30 and 11:00 p.m. When the call from Midland did not come through at 11:00, Dever said he left for the plant. He and a plant worker found Jasper Russell's body about 20 minutes past midnight.

Edith Shehan worked as a cashier at Midland. She described for the court how her office looked the morning after the crime. A window broken and a safe damaged—the safe that contained an envelope with Joe Weaver's name on it.

"The envelope is sent to me with the amount of money on the outside and I put the money in. That is all."[86]

Shehan said she had put $6.72 inside the envelope.

Jesse Schwab, a millwright at the plant, said he was at work when Thomas Dever arrived around 11:45 p.m. Schwab knew the route of the boxes that Russell had rung. The two of them found Russell's body about 100 feet from the carpenters' shop.

William Warren was employed as a Cleveland Railway Company conductor on the Madison Avenue line. He told the court that his car left Public Square at exactly 9:05. While he could not say what time his car had arrived at its destination, Rocky River, he recalled that at 9:05 the Defendant boarded the streetcar on the Square and got off at Berea Road and West 110th Street. The car was due to arrive at Berea Road at 9:32. Warren was uncertain whether someone was with the Defendant. But the Defendant was, the conductor said, the same man he had seen two days later in the lineup at the police station.

William Marsteller was the lead trial attorney. His southern drawl floated smoothly over the courtroom whenever he examined a witness or appealed to a jury.

On cross-examination by Marsteller, the witness could not tell the court exactly what time he went to work that night. Neither could he tell the total number of people that boarded his car at 9:05 at Public Square. He said he made three round trips before 9:05, and about three after. He could not say what time he left Public Square on the first two trips. He was certain only of the time he left the Square on the third trip, 9:05. He didn't know exactly what time he left on the fourth or the fifth trip. Asked about the sixth trip, "about twelve-something" was as close as Warren could come.

> "Now this third trip, mightn't it have been that it was nine-ten that you left the Public Square instead of nine-five?"
> "It was nine-five when I left," [said Warren.]
> "It was nine-five, but mightn't it have been nine-ten that you left the Public Square instead of nine-five?"
> "Nine-five."
> "What time on that trip at 9:05 did you arrive at Rocky River?"
> "I don't just know."[87]

Warren had no better answer for the next several questions, which were about the times of his arrival at Rocky River on any of his other trips. He also could not say how many Negroes rode with him on his first and second trips. But he did remember the third trip when those "fellows that got off at Berea Road" rode in his car. He didn't notice when they got on the car, only when they got off.

> "And how many other people did you notice when they got on the car at the Public Square?"
> "Those were the only ones."
> "Those were the only people you noticed when they got on the car at the Public Square?"
> "I didn't pay any attention, only the one."

"Only the one. You only noticed one man that got on the car at the Public Square at nine-five—that was your third trip?"

"Yes, sir."

"Did five, ten, fifteen, twenty, or what number of people get on?" [Marsteller asked.]

"I don't know exactly."[88]

Neither did the witness know whether any other "colored" persons boarded the car at 9:05. But he was positive that two persons got off the car at 9:32. Not 9:33, 9:34, or any other time.

"Now you say that you saw this fellow in a line up?"

"Yes, sir."

"At Police Station?"

"Yes, sir."

"How many were in that line-up?"

"Five."

"How many of them were as tall as he was?"

"He was the only one."

"Only tall one, wasn't he?"

"Yes, sir."[89]

Warren testified that he first learned of the crime when he read the newspaper on Tuesday, March 15th. That was about 10:00 or 11:00 p.m. But not until a detective visited him at the car barn did he reveal that he had seen the man he had read about. Later in his testimony, Warren corrected himself and said the police came to see him on Tuesday night instead of Monday, March 14th, at about 8:00 in the morning, and that he had seen the reward offered in the papers.

It was James Connell's courtroom style to talk low to strain the jury's ear. On re-direct examination, the assistant county prosecutor asked:

"Now who was it who first mentioned the time when the car left the Square, was it the officer or yourself?"

"Well, he had the time—the time when I was at the Square, picked out on the schedule."

"You mean that before the officer talked to you, from some other source he had found out the schedule of your car?"

"Yes, sir."[90]

Edward Stanton's assistant, James Connell recalled Jesse Schwab to the stand and showed him some hand tools. The witness identified them as the ones found near the safe on March 14th. They belonged to the Company, he said.

The state called for Jack Mansfield, another Cleveland Railway Company conductor. Mansfield said his car was going east on Madison Avenue and stopped at West 105th Street.

"And about what distance is there between West 106th Street, which is the corner of the plant and West 105th Street where you made this stop?"

"Oh, I should judge about 200 feet."

"Now then, approximately what time was it, to the best of your memory, when you arrived at West 105th Street, going east towards the Public Square that night?"

"About ten-thirty."

[Mansfield] testified that the Defendant got on the car there at that time, that another colored fellow was with him.

"Now when they got on your car at that point, did anyone else get on with them?"

"Yes, sir. There was about two or three, about three other passengers got on after they did."

The car arrived at Public Square at ten-fifty, then these two colored men got off at the Public Square. The next time he saw them was in the Police Station—that was on Tuesday, March 15th.

At this time, the prosecutor asked that Alex Maynor be brought into the Court room. [Marsteller objected to Mayner's presence, contending that Joe Weaver was not responsible for Alex Mayner's acts on that night, and denied that Joe was with Alex. Note: The incorrect spelling of Mayner's name, changed in the public record to Maynor, is reflected in the excerpts that follow.]

"I didn't think I had asked a question as yet," [said Connell.]

"But I object to bringing Alex Maynor into the courtroom while this witness is testifying."

[The court overruled the objection.]

"May I save an exception?" [Marsteller asked.]

"Let the record so show."

"Now, would you bring him in again, Mr. Bailiff," [said Connell.]

"Now, Mr. Mansfield, I will ask you whether the other colored man whom you say you saw with this Defendant, Joseph Weaver that night, is in this courtroom."

"Yes, sir," [Mansfield said to Connell.]

"I asked him [Connell] to caution him [Mansfield], and you took exception to it," [Marsteller said to the judge.]

"Overruled."

"May I save an exception?"

"Yes, sir."

"You said yes, did you?" [Connell asked Mansfield.]

"Yes, sir."

"Point him out, please."

"That gentleman standing up there."

"That indicates, for the record, the second Defendant in this action, Alex Maynor," [said the attorney for the state.] "You may take the witness."

"I will object to that statement, 'the second Defendant in this case,'" [Marsteller said.] "He is not a Defendant in this case whatsoever."

"He is named in this indictment, if you will look at it," [Connell snapped back.]

"Overruled."[91]

Marsteller fired off another exception before beginning his cross-examination. The state's witness, Mansfield, said two Negroes got on the car ahead of three white people. He had his records in the courtroom. Consulting them, the streetcar conductor said he left the Square at 9:30 and arrived at Rocky River at 10:12.

"Now that is correct. There is no guessing about that. That is a record, is it not?"

"That is right."

"So as not to be mistaken, did you leave Rocky River at ten-twelve, or did you arrive at Rocky River—"

"We left there at ten-twelve."

"Now, between the Public Square and Rocky River, do you check your time in between?"

"No, sir."

"You do not. Then, you got to the Public Square at ten-fifty?"

"Ten-fifty."

"That is not a guessed hour, but is a checked hour?"

"Yes, sir."

"And was ten-fifty the regular hour that you were to get there, that is, the scheduled hour?" Marsteller asked.

"Yes, sir."

"So then your run from Rocky River to the Public Square on that run was on time?"

"Yes, sir."

"Now, leaving Rocky River at ten-twelve, you arrived at 105th Street at ten-thirty?"

"About ten-thirty."

"That would be eighteen minutes?"

"Yes, sir."

"Can you tell this jury whether or not you are certain that this is the time that you arrived at 105th Street?"

"That is the time we arrived there."

"It couldn't have been as late as ten-thirty-five?"

"No, because we was on time."

"You were on time. It couldn't have been as early as ten-twenty-five?"

"No."

"You are certain that it was ten-thirty."

"Absolutely."

[The witness said he] had never seen Joe Weaver before that night. Never heard of the crime having been committed at the Midland Steel Products Company until Tuesday and when told by the detectives, and did not happen to read the newspaper on Monday.

"Mr. Mansfield, isn't it true that you received a letter from Mr. Kulas, the president, or one of the officers of the Midland Steel Products Company?"

"I did, about a week ago, I guess."

"Isn't it true that in that letter he congratulated you for identifying a man on the street car?"

"No, sir. He didn't say nothing about that matter."

"Isn't it true that he told you that if the man in that letter were convicted, that he would see to it that you got part of the reward that had been offered?"

"He didn't say nothing of the kind."

"Did you make a communication with him or to the Company?"

"I just wrote a letter to—"

"What did you write a letter to the Company about?"

"Well, I just asked them after I found out about it. Just wrote and asked them if I was entitled to it. I wanted to get a job down there, but I didn't really ask him for a job."

"Mr. Mansfield, isn't it true that you wrote to them, wanting to know if you were going to get part of the reward that had been published?"

"I said something to them, and then I asked them—I really didn't ask them for a job; I told them I would like a position."

"And you did in that letter also ask for part of the reward that had been published."

"I said I thought I was entitled to it."[92]

On re-direct examination by the state, Mansfield said that he read about the reward in an old newspaper he had found down in the cellar. He had been looking for a story in the newspaper. The name of the story he thought was *Vivian*.

The defense read a letter to the court dated March 25, 1927, and addressed to the president of Midland Steel.

> Dear Sir: In regards to the reward offered by you for the arrest and conviction of the slayers of your night watchman that was killed on March 13-1927. I am the conductor on the Madison line

that picked up the two colored men at West 105 St. and Madison on Sunday night March 13- and let them off at the Public Square, and I called to go down to police Headquarters and identify the ones I picked up. I had to go down on March 21-27 before the Grand Jury to testify against them and expect to have to go down for their trials and I will do all I can to help to convict them. I would appreciate it very much and be very thankful if I could get part of the reward offered by you. Yours truly, (signed) Jack M. Mansfield [address] Lakewood, Ohio.[93]

The state offered Orley May as a witness, the detective on duty when Joe Weaver was arrested. He had taken down the suspect's statement of his whereabouts between 7:00 the evening of March 13th and 6:00 the following morning. Judge Carpenter was handed the written account.

"Is this Joe Weaver's statement, is it?"

"Yes, conversation I had with him that he stated that he was home at eight p.m."

[May said that the Defendant had told him that] he left the house around 8:10, went to 38th Street, then to East 49th and got home a few minutes after 10:00 on March 13th, and went right to bed. When he got home, Scofield, a negroe [sic] who occupied the same room with him, was in bed. He went right to bed, got up at six o'clock the following morning and went to work.[94]

With the Defendant's turn to present witnesses, Marsteller called Evelyn Bedell to the stand. Mrs. Bedell lived on East 57th Street with her mother, brother, and three roomers. Joe Weaver also was living at her house. He occupied a room on the second floor with another roomer. She had known him (presumably Joe) about one year and he had been living at her house for about four or five weeks.

The witness said the first time she saw the Defendant the day of the murder was between 9:00 and 10:00 at night. She saw him at her home in her dining room, and she gave him his dinner. She fixed the time by having wound her clock at the time she went to bed and it was exactly eleven o'clock. As near as she could guess he had gone upstairs about an hour before she went to bed. He went upstairs and then came down again for a few minutes to get his lunch, which he wrapped up for the next day. He went back upstairs. He was alone and Mrs. Bedell was sitting in her living room. He said to her, "Mrs. Bedell, say, I'm going to get the rest of that I left."

"He had bought a chicken and my mother had cooked it Sunday morning. He ate part of it and went upstairs and came back for the rest of the chicken for his lunch the next day. He took the lunch, wrapped up, upstairs with him."[95]

The landlady said she guessed the Defendant went upstairs for the last time around 10:00. From where she had sat in the living room, her view of the front stairway was unobstructed.

Mrs. Bedell said she did not see him come down again after 10:00. She said again that she had sat up until 11:00, when she wound up her clock and went to bed, and that as far as she knew, he did not come downstairs again that night. There were two other people in the room with her that night. And yes, the statement she now made was that which she had told to the detectives.

On cross-examination, Mrs. Bedell said her mother, brother, "the kid," and three roomers lived at her house. The kid was her husband's sister's child, a five-year-old. The detectives had taken the child and Mrs. Bedell to the police station.

"And did the officers say anything to her?" [the assistant prosecutor asked.]
"Yes."
"What did she say to them?"
"I object," [Marsteller broke in.] "Joe wasn't present. What the five-year-old said to the officers was out of Joe's presence."
After discussion by the Court and Counsel, the Court [said]:
"Objection overruled."

"May I save an exception to that, Your Honor?" [the defense attorney asked].

"Now what did the little girl say to the officer?"

"When they had taken her to the Police Station, they asked her had she seen Joe with a gun, with a revolver."

"What did she say?"

"She first said 'Yes' and then she said 'No.'"

"Well, now, when she said yes, what else did she say?"

"'I don't know.'"

"Did you hear what else she said?"

"That is what the kid said: 'I don't know.'"

"After the kid told the officers something about Joe and a gun, what did you say to the kid?"

"I said, 'Tell the truth.'"

"Isn't this the fact: Didn't the kid say there was a revolver underneath the bathtub in your bathroom? And didn't you tell her to keep her mouth shut? And didn't she then say that there wasn't?"

"No, I did not."

"That didn't happen that way?"

"No."

"This conversation was in your own home, wasn't it?"

"It was not."

"Where was it?"

"It was in the detective—it was in police central station."

"When was the first time that the officers came there?" [the state asked].

"They came there on a Tuesday morning."

"Where did they go?"

"They went upstairs to Weaver's bedroom."[96]

The defense called its next witness, Emil Bokson, a Romanian employed at Midland. Bokson's broken English necessitated interpretation. Through the interpreter, Emil, a gypsy, said he knew the Defendant, as well as Alex Mayner and wife, Viola. The day of the murder Bokson and his wife were visited by Alex and Viola and another couple. His guests arrived around 3:00 or 4:00

in the afternoon. They drank wine. The two colored women, he said, got drunk, consuming about three or five gallons of wine before they left his house after 8:00. He took off his clothes and went to bed around 9:15, 15 to 30 minutes after Mayner left.

"Will you ask this question, please?" [Marsteller asked the interpreter.] "When Alex came to your house, did he say anything to you about your money?"

[That drew an objection from Stanton's assistant, sustained by the Bench.]

"What conversation did you have with Alex when he came to your house?"

[Connell registered another objection and was again sustained.]

"What if anything was said by Alex to you about money?"

"Objection."

[This time, Judge Carpenter asked Connell the nature of his objection.]

"I think it ought to be possible to put a question that isn't leading," [Connell groused.]

"That is the objection, is it?"

"Yes, Your Honor. I object on the grounds that it is not collateral anyhow."

"That is the thing that is concerning me more than the leading character," [said the court.]

"It is part of the attack of Alex Maynor's own testimony," [Marsteller said.]

"You asked him and he said no," [Connell shot back.]

"If I laid ground for impeachment of his testimony—"

"We are objecting to it on the grounds that it is a purely collateral issue," [the assistant prosecutor interjected.]

"We are not trying Alex Maynor at this time," [the court said.]

"We are showing Alex Maynor's motive, and the question was asked him on cross-examination and foundation was laid," [Marsteller argued.]

"Being collateral matter, I submit that they are bound by the answer," [said Connell.]

"Sustained."

[Marsteller registered another exception in order to document what he saw as the trial court's error in overruling his objections.]

"May I read in the record what our witness would say? If the witness were permitted to testify, he would testify that Alex Maynor asked him if he had any money; that he replied to Alex Maynor that he had about eight thousand dollars, and Alex Maynor asked him where he kept his money, and he told Alex Maynor that he kept all of his money in the bank and none in the house."[97]

Upon adjournment the Defendant was returned to the filth and moral degradation of county jail. A makeshift diary became the repository of his emotional distress. One jail experience that he noted seemed more like Tony Colletti's description three years later than the "novel third degree" dished out in newsprint the month before: "The third degree is just a living killing. They leave enough breath in the body to stand trial and that's all. They takes a piece of hose and beats you and bats your head against the wall."[98]

Reportedly, the state's case received a severe jolt on Wednesday when its key witness refused to testify; however, the next day on the witness stand, Alex Mayner said:

"That's Joe Weaver, the man who shot Jasper Russell to death."

[After describing how he and his accomplice committed the crime, Mayner] was asked to point out Weaver. He did dramatically. Weaver stared at him without the slightest show of emotion.[99]

Alex testified that Joe Weaver came to his house and to his room, about noon on March 13th.

"Well, he commenced talking about the Company had done shortchanged him of six dollars. I didn't know nothing about that."

[Marsteller expressed displeasure with Mayner's words. His objection was overruled.]

"And he told me if I come and go with him, he knowed where he could get, get some money. Well, I set and—"

[The defense interrupted again, and again was overruled.]

"I set and studies awhile—"

[Again Mayner was interrupted by the opposing attorney whose objection was overruled.]

"'Sure,' and he says, 'I will call back by here tonight if you say you come, come and go.' And so I finally answered him 'yes.'"

"Did he say anything else at that time about where you would go?"

"Well, he said he would go out there, go out there at this plant."

"And what else did he say about the plant, if anything?" [the prosecutor asked.]

"Well, he goes ahead: then we goes out there."

[Mayner was directed to confine his narrative for the time being to what took place at his room.]

"Well, just only he said he knowed where this safe was."

"Was there any more said then?"

"And then he said if I come, if I come and go, he had a revolver for retection [sic]."

[The defense objected and was overruled.]

"Did Joe Weaver say anything else at that time that you remember at this time?"

"No. Only he got his coat and hat and left."

"And did you say anything else?"

"No."[100]

Mayner further testified that the Defendant had called for him that night between 9:00 and 10:00. The two of them, he said, took the streetcar out to the plant, each paying his fare and sitting apart. They left the streetcar a short distance from the plant, walked to the plant, and climbed over the high wire fence. He said he got a ladder from the premises, and Joe got a hammer and other tools from someplace. Mayner went on to say:

Weaver used the ladder to climb up to the window of the office, broke the window with the hammer, unfastened the latch, raised the window, and climbed in. Of his further participation

Maynor says, "I, I clum up there and set down on the windowsill and that, that's fur as I went."[101]

Alex stated that while he sat on the windowsill, Weaver tried to open the safe. After working on the safe for about half an hour, Weaver said he heard the night watchman approaching. Mayner jumped out the window, Weaver behind him.

"Well, now, when you got down to run, did you say anything to Joe or did Joe say anything to you?"

"Well, he says he will go up there and stash himself there at this water house."

[This drew an objection from the defense, which was overruled.]

"Did he say anything further about where you were to go or not?"

"Well, he says, he says, 'You go, you go on down behind that, behind that there car shop.'"

Maynor testified that he ran down behind the car shop and that Weaver ran behind the water house; that, as the night watchman approached, Weaver shot him, and the night watchman fell.

"Could you tell whether he was lying face down or not?" Connell asked.

"Well, well, I couldn't tell exactly whether his face was down, but it seemed like to me, yes, he was laying on his face."

"What did you see Weaver do then after the watchman was found?"

"Then, then after, after he made the second shot, why, he steps up and commences, commences to search him."

"And when you say 'commenced to search', tell us just what you mean so that we won't misunderstand you. How did he search?"

"He commenced going, going into his pockets."

"And then what did he do?"

"He got out one, one little, one little black pocketbook that I could see from the distance that I was standing off from him."

"How far from Weaver were you?"

"I was, I was about fifteen, I was a little bettern fifteen foot from him."

[The defense objected.]

"How many pocketbooks did you see him get?"

"One."

"That is all you saw?"

"That is all," said Maynor. "That is all I saw, but after they done rested me over to the police station why the officer showed two."

"Then you saw two?"

"Sure."

"But that night all you saw was one?"

"One."

"Did you see what Weaver did with them?"

"No, I don't."

[The defense objected again and was overruled.]

"Did Weaver say anything about that pocketbook?"

"Well, after he gets the pocketbook he says, 'Here, here's two little tickets.' Well, at that time I breaks into a run to leave then."[102]

Maynor testified that Weaver was close behind him climbing the fence, and that he caught his coat on the barbed wire and tore a piece out of the coat. They boarded a streetcar. He paid his own fare, and, sitting apart, they rode back downtown and went their separate ways.

[Marsteller, the law professor who thrived on courtroom give-and-take, cross-examined Alex Mayner.] He began by asking the state's witness about the Romanian, Emil Bokson.

"Alex, when you got over to the gypsy's house, isn't it true that you asked the gypsy if he had any money?"

"Did I ask the gypsy that?"

"Yes."

"I did not."

"And didn't he tell you he had about 8,000 dollars."

"Naw."

"And didn't you ask him where he kept it?"

"I did not."

"And didn't he tell you that he kept it in the bank?"

"I did not. I did not."

"And didn't you go over to the gypsy's that night to rob the gypsy?"

"I did not, I did not. I did not go over to that gypsy's to rob him."

"And you say now that you had no conversation with the gypsy whatever in regard to the money the gypsy had?"

[Connell objected.] "He said he didn't, and you heard him."

"He may answer," [the court said.]

[It was Connell's turn to register an exception.]

"I did not," [Alex Mayner said.][103]

The defense called for Frank J. McGraw to testify. The Defendant's witness identified himself as a timekeeper at Midland Steel Products. He reported that he had known the Defendant as an employee of the Company for more than three and a half years and had kept a record of the Defendant's work.

"Mr. McGraw, when Alex left the Company, do you know about how much money he was earning per day?"

"Objection to the question unless it is corrected to mean Weaver."

"I mean Joe Weaver."

"Objection to the question with the correction."

"Sustained."

"Do I understand I cannot show by the chief timekeeper who would have the knowledge as to how much he was earning?" [Marsteller asked.]

"No."

"May I have an exception then to it and may I read into the record?"

Thereupon Counsel for the Defendant offered to prove that if the witness were permitted to answer he would testify that Joe Weaver was making fifteen dollars a day at the time he quit working [at Midland].[104]

The defense called Mrs. Lucretia Cook to the stand. She was living with her daughter, Evelyn Bedell, where the Defendant also lived. She testified that she saw the Defendant on March 13th in the morning and that night. Mrs. Cook, who could not tell time, was asked:

> "And where was he when you saw him Sunday night?"
> "He came in the door and come on in a little hall, little hall as wide as from that chair here where he had to go to eat his supper."
> She saw him eat his supper Sunday night, her daughter fixed the supper, after he ate his supper he went upstairs, [Mrs. Cook] washed the dishes, cleaned up the kitchen and went to bed. She saw him no more that night. Did not know what time she went to bed.[105]

George Johnson had known the Defendant since 1923. Called to testify, he said he had seen the Defendant quite often and that they knew the same people.

> "Now what kind of a reputation does he enjoy with regard to being a law abiding citizen?"
> "Well, as far as I know of his reputation and from people that know him, I know about him, he has an excellent reputation— Was at my house on Sunday, March 13th."[106]

When Johnson left his house at 7:30, Weaver was still there. He remembered the time because he looked at his watch and started for church.

Hattie Johnson, his wife, was called to testify and said that she had known the Defendant for three or four years. She said she left Joe Weaver at the house at 7:30 when she left with her husband. She added:

> "Oh, the people said that he was law abiding citizen, so far as I know of, everybody gave him that for the people that I can recommend—they gives him very, very good reputation."[107]

Next to testify for the defense was Nettie Pope. She too had known Joe Weaver about four years. He came to her house on Sunday, March 13.

> "My daughter was going to the church and I said to her, 'If you going to church,' I said, 'If you going to church, why it will be too late.' And she said, 'No, it ain't.' Then her husband pulled out the watch and he says, 'It is half after seven now.' I sat there a good while, right smart a little bit, and after a while he went out." Defendant was there after her daughter and husband went to church.[108]

John Scofield took the stand for the defense. He said he first met the Defendant at Evelyn Bedell's house and they shared a bedroom there. On Sunday, March 13th, he came home at 9:00 or quarter past. Weaver was in their room. They exchanged a few words. Scofield said he went to bed about 9:45 while Weaver was going in and out of the room. Asked the time he last saw Joe Weaver that night, Scofield replied, "Well, I figure pretty close to 10:00."

The police had his statement.[109]

Dan Hall testified that he knew the Defendant, that the Defendant had come to his house on Sunday night, March 13th, and stayed about ten minutes, leaving, he said, "about twenty minutes to nine."[110]

The Defendant offered Hall's wife as a witness. She testified that Joe Weaver had come to their house on Sunday night, March 13th, and that was her first time ever seeing him. She said he came about 8:30 and stayed about 20 minutes, leaving "about ten minutes to nine."[111]

Fannie Siler testified. She said she was at the Halls' house that Sunday night and had seen the Defendant, but did not know him. After pointing him out in the courtroom, she said the Defendant came to the house about 8:30, and stayed there "about ten minutes."[112]

Granderson Cross was sworn in. He had known the Defendant 15 years or so, once living at Joe's house for six or seven months.

The Defendant and he were from the same part of Georgia and had worked as a team at Midland. Judge Carpenter said what mattered was whether the Defendant's reputation both before and after coming to Cleveland was good or bad.

"It was good," Cross answered.[113]

Jesse Levy, on the witness stand, said he knew the Defendant when he saw him, but did not know him personally. He had seen the Defendant on Sunday night, March 13th, at Evelyn Bedell's house. That was after 9:00, he said, but could not be exact.[114]

Next to testify was Joseph Bennett who had known the Defendant in Georgia. From age eight, he had been raised with Weaver. Bennett said he had been in Cleveland five years and had associated with the Defendant in this city also. Bennett confirmed Weaver's good reputation.[115]

The defense called for the Defendant's brother, Charley Weaver, a Baptist preacher like their father. The Defendant enjoyed a good reputation in Georgia, Charley said.[116]

Sister Susie Smith had also come to testify and be at her younger brother's side. On the witness stand, she was asked about her brother's reputation. Susie said her brother was well-spoken of in Georgia "among the whites as well as the coloreds."[117]

The defense called for Orrie Weaver. Joe's estranged wife testified that they had married in Waynesboro, Georgia, in 1919, and that she had come with him to Cleveland. They had separated, she said, on February 7, 1927. Still she affirmed his good reputation.[118]

Susan Lodge testified that she had lived in Cleveland about four years and came from Midville, Georgia. She said she had known the Defendant all his life, had known his mother and father, and that she had been the same as a mother to him. She had helped to raise him.

"He enjoyed a fine life, good recommendation, all where he lived."[119]

The Defendant took the witness stand. He said he was 33 years of age, and gave an account of his life up to the time he came to Cleveland and was hired as a spray painter at Midland Steel. He said that he and his partner were painting 500 frames a day at the time he quit the plant, and they were paid three cents a frame. The two of them left the Company because their rate was cut. It was very hard work and the Defendant considered it too hard for the money paid after his rate was cut. He and his partner quit at the same time.

When he quit, he told the chief timekeeper, Mr. McGraw, that the company had not paid him all he believed was due him. McGraw told him to figure out what was owed and mail his figures to the Company. He did that and received a reply on March 11th. It began "Dear Friend Joe," and informed him that a check had been done on the shortage he was alleging. According to McGraw's records, Joe had made a dollar error.

> "Another error on your part is two hundred and three Jordan frames times four cents each equals $9.12, whereas the correct amount is $8.12. However, I have found a shortage for you of $6.72 which you can get at any time."[120]

The Defendant said the day his wife left him he went to live on East 57th Street and shared a room with John Scofield. Judge Carpenter refused to allow him to tell the court why his wife had left him. He went on to say that he had sold clothing, taking measurements and orders at night and on Sundays. On Sunday morning, March 13th, he said he got up "a bit after 10:00," and set out to take orders. He went to Alex Mayner's house, a place he had never been before. He told Alex that he had quit his job at Midland and that McGraw had said he had $6.72 coming and could pick it up at any time.

> "Then Alex said, 'Well, Joe, I am almost ready to let you order that cloth for the old lady to make her that suit.'
> "So I run my hand in my pocket and take out a piece of paper and I wrote my address on East 57th Street and I gave it to him. And told him, I said, 'Well, Alex, when you get ready to order that suit, this is my number. You can come 'round there and I will order that cloth for your wife.'

"This talk took place out in the hall because Alex's wife was dressing in her room. Then she came out, said she was ready to go to church, and we could come in the room.

"I went on in the door there and I said, 'Alex, I stopped by for that little article, that gun that you had taken from my house February the seventh.'

"Alex said, 'Joe, it was a man here yesterday and we was looking at your gun and he wanted to buy it from me and I told him that it wasn't mine and I couldn't sell it. I told him it belong to a fellow by the name of Joe Weaver, and he had moved and I did not know his address. He said it was a white man and a colored man that hauls whisky from Canada to Cleveland once a week. And he said he wanted a good gun. I told him if I knew your address that I would get in his car and go around to see you and probably could make a trade with you and I could sell him this gun.'

"I says, 'Yes, Alex,' and he said, 'Joe, if you leave this gun here with me, I will see that man tonight or tomorrow and I can get twenty-five dollars for it.'

"I told him, I says, 'Well, Alex, if you can get twenty-five dollars for the gun, that is seven dollars more than I paid for it.' I says, 'I bought it about two years ago, which I ordered from New York,' I says, 'I am not housekeeping now. I am rooming and I don't need no gun.' I says, 'Now if you can sell it for twenty-five dollars, you sell it.'"[121]

Joe testified that he left the gun at Mayner's house around 12:30 and did not see Alex anymore that day or night. He didn't see Mayner until Tuesday, March 15th, and that was at the police station.

From Alex's house the Defendant said he went to his home on East 57th Street. He changed into a pin-striped suit, left at 3:00, and went over to Lonnie Gregory's house on East 43rd Street. From there he went to East 39th Street where Hattie Johnson and Nettie Pope lived. He stayed there until 7:30 or so, then left and headed west on East 35th Street, intending to see his wife. By the time he got to Woodland and East 39th, it was raining very hard, so he got on the streetcar and went to Central and East 55th Street.

He got off there and went into a store and bought a bottle of milk, arriving home about 8:00. The store was about 200 yards from where he lived. He was in the house about 10 minutes, then left and went to Dan Hall's house. It took him about 10 or 15 minutes to get there. He said he stayed there about 10 or 15 minutes. He got back to Mrs. Bedell's house about 9:00.

Mrs. Bedell fixed his dinner and he ate it. Her mother came in and said,

> "If you go out and get yourself some lunch biscuits, the part of the chicken you have left will make you a lunch for tomorrow."
> [Joe told the court that he went out, taking the bottle back to the store for his deposit.]
> "I had another bottle already and I bought the lunch biscuits with it."[122]

The Defendant said he went back to the same store on the corner of 57th Street. He returned to Mrs. Bedell's and went upstairs. He made out the papers for the orders for clothing he had taken that week. When he went upstairs it was between 9:00 and 9:30. No one was in the room. While he was working on the orders John Scofield came in. Joe had his papers on Scofield's bed.

> "'Well, John, I will make room for you. I am in your way.' Scofield said, 'All right. You are not in my way.' And so I finished writing those orders right then. And that is about all I did at that time."[123]

Joe said he went downstairs and wrapped up the chicken, his lunch for the next day. He was in the kitchen about 10 minutes. He went through the dining room and through the room where Evelyn Bedell was sitting and went right upstairs. When he got upstairs, it was about 10:00 and he told Scofield that he was back.

> "Scofield grunted, 'Un-huh.'"

Scofield seemed about "three-fourths asleep," [by Joe Weaver's calculation.] He was covered up, and Joe did not disturb his him.

"I stripped off, pulled off my clothes and 10 minutes after 10 I winds up my Hampden watch and my alarm clock to wake me up at six the next morning. And I got into bed and there I stayed until I got up the next morning at six o'clock and walks all the way down to Hydraulic and works all day that day."

[Note: The following is a simplification of Marsteller's argument before the appeals court.]

Joe was sure that he went to bed at 10:10 because he wound his watch and fixed his alarm clock at that time—fixed his alarm clock to wake him up at 6:00, worked an hour overtime at Hydraulic on Monday, March 14th, and left there about 5:00 or 5:30, got home Monday night about 7:00—that is, Evelyn Bedell's house, got up next morning, Tuesday morning, and went back to work a few minutes after 7:00. While at work, the detectives came out to him on the job, and came up back and slipped the handcuffs on him.

He was not west of the Square on Sunday night, March 13th. While he was working at the Midland Steel Products, he always went from 57th Street to work on the street car, taking a west bound Central car to the Public Square. That would take about 20 minutes. From the Square, he would take a Madison car west and get off at 105th or 110th and Madison. That would take up 30 minutes on the street car. It would take him from where he roomed on E. 57th Street to the plant of the Midland Steel Products about 50 minutes to an hour by street car. He could not make it much less than an hour because he would have to wait for a street car at the Square and lose some time. Usually, he left about 5:50 in the morning and would get to the factory a few minutes before 7:00.

"Joe," [Marsteller said,] "on March the 13th of this year, Sunday, around twelve to one o'clock or at any time, did you have any conversation with Alex Maynor in regard to going to the Midland Steel Products Company's plant and breaking open the safe?"

"No, sir, I never thought of nothing like that, never tried to make attempt even to take nothing from nobody—ain't got a drop of that kind of blood in me."[124]

"Were you in the Army," [asked Marsteller.]

"Yes, sir," [Weaver replied.]

"And were you discharged from the Army?"

"Yes, sir."

"I ask this to be marked for identification."

The court reporter received the Defendant's Army discharge paper, Exhibit D.

"To which we object, Your Honor," [said the prosecuting attorney], "as it has no part in the defense in this case. We didn't object to the question that he had been in the Army because we wanted to be fair, but I don't think that is material as a defense to this charge."

The court sustained the objection and overruled the defense's exception request.

"May I save an exception? Did you get an honorable discharge from the Army?"

"Objection."

The objection was again sustained. Another exception request followed.[125]

On rebuttal, the state called Joseph Jacobs, a detective who was present when Joe Weaver was brought to Evelyn Bedell's house after his arrest at work on the morning of March 13, 1927.

"At the time that you were there, did you have occasion to see a young child come into the house?"

"What was that? This is rebuttal," [said Marsteller.]

"But I have to put him somewhere to make rebuttal. Can't put it all in one question or you could object to that."

"Did you get the question?"

"No," Marsteller replied to the judge.

[The question was read, after which the court overruled the objection.]

"Exception. And may I state to the court my reason for my objection?"

"Privately, surely," [said Connell.]

"What is your answer to that question?"

"We were at the child's house where Weaver lived," [the detective replied.]

"Did you see Evelyn Bedell at that time?" [the prosecuting attorney asked.]

"Well, that wasn't on the 15th."

"When was it?"

"That was about on the 16th."

"I see. Did you see Evelyn Bedell at that time?"

"The day we walked into the—. Were going to go into this house, the child was on the porch with roller skates."

[Marsteller interrupted the state and exchanged heated sarcasm with Connell. The state resumed questioning.]

"Did you see Evelyn Bedell and a child close together at any time?"

"Child came to the door right following us up while we were walking in."

[Marsteller interrupted again. Connell continued to question Jacobs.]

"When you went in, what, if anything, did the child say to Mrs. Bedell, and what, if anything, did Mrs. Bedell say to the child?"

"I object, Your Honor."

"Overruled."

"Exception. I wish the record to show that I make an objection at this time, that the Defendant was not present."

"Overruled."

"Exception."

"The child says, 'You want that gun that was found under the tub?'"

"The child said that to who?"

"She said it to nobody in particular. She says, 'Are you after that?' and possibly referred to us. I would take it so."

"Who was there?"

"The child said, 'Are you after the gun that was found under the tub?'"

"And what, if anything, did Evelyn Bedell say?"

"'Oh, you keep quiet', and said to us, 'She don't know what she's talking about.'"[126]

90

William Marsteller closed out the defense's case late on the fifth day of trial. He depicted his client as a victim of a frame-up by Alex Mayner. The state, in its final argument, demanded a verdict of guilty, which carried with it the penalty of death in the electric chair. Judge Irving Carpenter charged the jury on a first-degree murder verdict only—nothing less. The jury was led out of the courtroom.

Four hours later, at 10:30 that evening, the buzzer in the courtroom sounded, signaling that a verdict had been reached. The visiting judge was summoned from his hotel room.

The jurors filed into the courtroom, white-faced and solemn. The Defendant was brought in, handcuffed to the deputy sheriff, his attorneys behind him. He took his seat at the left side of the defense table. His wife Orrie and sister Susie were seated behind him.

"Ladies and gentlemen of the jury, have you reached a verdict?"

"We have, Your Honor."

The Defendant showed no emotion as the deputy county clerk read the verdict: We, the jury in this case being duly impaneled and sworn, do find the Defendant, Joseph Weaver, guilty of murder in the first degree as charged in the indictment.

His head bowed, Joe mumbled a prayer as handcuffs were again snapped on him.

Stanton's assistant told reporters he was satisfied that justice had been done.

Patting his client on the back, Marsteller said:

"Don't you worry, Joe....We know you're innocent and we'll see that you get a square deal and get out of this."[127]

Tears rolled down Orrie's cheeks at the fate of her estranged husband. Susie, who had gone from praying on the courthouse steps to doing the same in front of the judge's bench, wailed as her baby brother was led away in handcuffs. The foreman told news reporters that the jury had taken four ballots before agreeing to convict.

"There was no separate vote taken on the mercy clause. We agreed that if Weaver was guilty, he deserved the chair," the spokesman said. "The evidence showed that the killing was absolutely cold-blooded and brutal."[128]

Back in the Black Hole, Joe Weaver, morose and disinclined to talk, was under heavy guard in the section reserved for convicted killers. On the third day after courtroom proceedings (for which their client was billed $349.15), Cook and Marsteller filed a motion for a new trial. Judge Carpenter agreed to hear the motion on the following Saturday.

The trial of Alex Mayner, the state's star witness, began on April 18th, the same day the Weaver appeal was filed. After meeting with his attorneys, Judge Carpenter, and Prosecutors Stanton and Connell, Alex—in his testimony on the stand—owned up to his part in the murder of Jasper Russell. He was sentenced to life without parole. The court explained that clemency had been shown because of this Defendant's invaluable assistance in convicting Joe Weaver. The accuser was in the penitentiary before the week ended.

In their appeal to the common pleas judge, Cook and Marsteller claimed Prosecutor Edward Stanton had acted in deliberate bad faith. According to them, the prosecutor had failed to produce a witness the defense deemed crucial to its case. This inaction, they said, compromised the fairness of the trial because they had not been allowed to subpoena that witness. They said Stanton had promised a week before the trial to bring in a relative of Alex Mayner, and had repeated the promise during the trial. Allegedly, Stanton told Cook a detective had been sent to bring in the man known to have some valuable knowledge of the case. When asked about the witness, the detective simply laughed, Cook said in the motion.[129]

Stanton responded to the complaint by explaining that the witness had been in the corridor but was not called to the stand.

Judge Carpenter set a date for ruling on the motion—Tuesday, April 26, at 4:00. At that time he would either order a new trial based on newly discovered evidence, or set the date of electrocution. The two court-assigned lawyers informed the judge that they were willing to serve without charge, if need be, should the court grant a new trial.

On April 26, Judge Carpenter overruled the motion for a new trial. With the defense registering an exception to his decision he went on to the next order of the day.

"Do you have anything to say as to why judgment should not be pronounced against you?" the judge asked the condemned man.

"I have only this to say, Your Honor. That if you sentence me, you will be sending an innocent man to his death. I know nothing about the crime, and I don't think I got justice on the jury."[130]

"It is considered and adjudged by the court that the Defendant, Joseph Weaver, be taken to the jail of Cuyahoga County, and within the next 30 days the sheriff of Cuyahoga County convey the said Joseph Weaver to the Ohio Penitentiary at Columbus, Ohio, and deliver him to the warden of the said Penitentiary, and that he be there safely kept until the twelfth day of August, 1927 on which day within an enclosure inside the walls of the Ohio Penitentiary prepared for that purpose, according to law, the said Defendant, Joseph Weaver, shall be electrocuted by the warden of the Ohio Penitentiary,...that said warden or his duly appointed deputy shall cause to pass through the body of said Joseph Weaver a current of electricity of sufficient intensity to cause death, and the application of such current of electricity shall be continued by said warden of said penitentiary or said deputy as aforesaid until the said Defendant, Joseph Weaver, is dead. And that the said Defendant pay the cost of this prosecution for which execution is awarded."[131]

Susie Smith sobbed as her handcuffed brother quietly followed the deputy sheriff out of the courtroom. On April 29th, he was transported from the Black Hole on the Square to the big house in Columbus. The month ended with 71-year-old Mary Russell closing her eyes in death. Either consumption or a broken heart had ended her life, depending on which family member was asked.

CHAPTER 8

WEST SPRING STREET

More than 2,500 inmates populated the 24-acre limestone compound on West Spring Street the day the convicted killer of Jasper Russell arrived under escort and in chains. His passage through the turnstile augmented the prison's black population— at 31 percent the preceding year. The handcuffs came off before he was led through another set of gates and out into the yard.

Still smarting from the third degree, he nonetheless walked with unfaltering footsteps, a guard escorting him to the deputy warden's office. There he was searched and assigned inmate number 57064. Next he was taken to the commissary and issued a prison uniform. A bath followed, and finally his return to the deputy's office for assignment to death row.

Locked up in a 7½ foot by five-foot cell, for a while Joe had no appetite for food, and sleep eluded him. He turned to his confidant, the make-do diary carried from county jail. (Writing down important things was a practice probably carried over from his sharecropping days.)

"The strain it is to suffer the death sentence for what another person done, and know where he is, and know that he has lied and slipped his trick offen you and you can't get to him to wring his neck!"[132]

95

A few days after his arrival on death row mail came. There was a letter forwarded from county jail. It bore the signature of the executive secretary of the Negro Welfare Association of Cleveland, an affiliate of the National Urban League. [The League began its fight against racial discrimination in the North in 1910.]

> My Dear Mr. Weaver: We have your letter of a few days ago and regret to state that there is nothing we can do in your case. The Courts have decided that you must pay the penalty for the offense.
>
> We are glad to hear you say that you are innocent. Other innocent men have suffered for offenses of which they were not guilty. We hope that in some way your innocence will become known before it is too late.
>
> Yours truly,
>
> (signed) William R. Conners[133]

On May 26th, Joe's lawyers, in the role of Plaintiffs against the state, took their fight to the court of appeals. Courtroom procedure errors were alleged in the brief they filed with the court. Cook and Marsteller charged that the jury had sentenced their client to death simply because Alex Mayner had said Joe Weaver was his accomplice. Challenging the credibility of that witness, they claimed Alex Mayner was under such a nervous strain that he, unlike their client, could not go to work the morning after the crime. As for the man they represented, they said in their appeal:

> Joe Weaver, the man whom Maynor claimed to be his accomplice in the commission of the murder, was at his work, worked all day, went to his work the second day, and in the morning of the second day was arrested by the officers while at work.
>
> Joe Weaver enjoyed a good reputation for honesty and integrity, had never been arrested or inside of a police station in his life, was a hard worker, making $15 a day, and a man whose record for decent living ought not to be swept away and his life

snuffed out in the electric chair by the putrid breath of a self-asserted accomplice, a conspirator and a self-confessed burglar and murderer, without corroborating testimony....[134]

The attorneys pointed to their client's lack of hesitation in telling the police exactly where he was when the crime was committed. At no time was he within seven miles of the murder scene.

> The state caused Joe Weaver to be tried first and on the uncorroborated testimony of Alex Maynor the jury sent Joe Weaver to the electric chair. After the jury brought in their verdict, Alex Maynor pled guilty and was sentenced to life imprisonment, which leads us to believe was in accordance with a promise, either expressed or implied, made by the prosecutor of Cuyahoga County with counsel for Alex Maynor, providing that if he testified and made a case against Joe Weaver, the saving of his own life would be his reward.
>
> We, as attorneys for this indigent prisoner, after days and nights of investigation, and since the verdict, after months of thought, study and further investigation, respectfully say to this Court that Joe Weaver had no connection whatsoever with this crime and that an absolutely innocent man is being sent to the electric chair.
>
> We maintain the jury found its verdict solely upon the evidence of the self-asserted accomplice, through passion and prejudice, and that the record in this case does not show an iota of corroborating testimony of this self-asserted accomplice.[135]

The attorneys argued that Joe Weaver did not get a fair trial, errors were committed in the admission of evidence and in the trial judge's ruling on such evidence, and that verdict was against the weight of the evidence and contrary to law.

One error called prejudicial by the Plaintiffs involved the conversation of Evelyn Bedell, her young niece, and the officer. The accused was not present when that conversation took place. Since the state had no testimony to corroborate Alex Mayner's story, it tried to make the jury believe a gun was found in the house after Joe was arrested.

> And such prejudicial error had the desired effect upon the jury. Further, in permitting any testimony about what the child had told the police officer with the Defendant absent, Judge Carpenter also committed error.[136]

Added to that error was the testimony of Emil Bokson. The Romanian had been put on the stand to show that Alex Mayner had intended to rob Bokson. His interpreted testimony was vital because it revealed that Mayner and a man named Martin had come to Emil's house that afternoon and stayed until 8:30 or so. During that time about four gallons of wine had been consumed.

> ...The wives of these two Negroes became very drunk. The two Negro men themselves drank very little wine.[137]

[Note: The following is a simplification of Marsteller's argument before the appeals court.]

Maynor had worked with Bokson as a helper and knew Bokson had money. In the Plaintiffs' view, Maynor and Martin intended to get the women so drunk they would know nothing about their husbands' doings and whereabouts that Sunday night. The Plaintiffs argued that the testimony about Bokson's money—whether he had any and where he kept it—was competent evidence. Had it been allowed, the Romanian's testimony would have shown that Maynor intended to rob someone that night, he and Martin together; that it was Martin and not the Defendant, Joe Weaver, who was with Alex Maynor at the time Maynor committed the burglary and the murder.

Procedural error was allegedly committed when the court did not permit the witness to answer after the defense challenged Maynor's testimony.

Emil Bokson's testimony would have clarified to the jury Maynor's plans for that afternoon and evening. Furthermore, from the time Maynor left Bokson's house by car, he would not have had time to meet Weaver and go by streetcar out to Midland, leaving the Square at 9:05. [Marsteller went on to say:]

> On the contrary, [the jury] would have seen how plausible it was for Alex Maynor and Martin to have deposited their wives and to have gone in an automobile to Madison and West 106th Street, and to have committed the crime.[138]

Another prejudicial error allegedly occurred when the court disallowed the timekeeper to tell how much money the Defendant had been earning at the plant.

> It was the state's case that the Defendant went with Alex Maynor…to secure six or seven dollars that the company owed Joe Weaver. It certainly is most important as a matter of defense to show that Joe Weaver was making big money—namely, $15.00 per day—for it is not likely that a Negro man making $15.00 per day is likely to go out to rob a safe when he knows nothing about opening a safe…. Those working on that safe that night could have worked for a week with the tools they had, and in the manner they were going about the work, they could not have gotten the safe door open….
>
> A man who is charged with first degree murder has a right to show to the Jury his general reputation for being a law abiding citizen…. An honorable discharge from the Army, after having served in the World War, would certainly be the best evidence in regard to a man's reputation as a law-abiding citizen. The only reward that a man gets for serving his country is an honorable discharge…and it is the first time in the history of the courts that a prosecuting attorney has objected to the accused showing his honorable discharge. We believe that if the jury had been permitted to know that the Defendant had been honorably discharged, the jury would have given more credence to Joe Weaver's testimony, and would have been more inclined to realize that a man of his type was incapable of [committing] the crime of which he was accused.[139]

In the Plaintiffs' view, not an iota of testimony existed to implicate Joe Weaver aside from Alex Mayner's words.

On the contrary, witness after witness testified that Joe Weaver was in their presence seven miles from the scene of the crime at or about the time the crime was committed. Alex Maynor testified that he and his accomplice did not wear gloves while they were handling the tools, working on the safe, breaking the window and opening the window. The tools were found lying near the safe and the State failed to show any fingerprints or marks either upon the tools, upon the metal safe, or upon the glass of the window. It stands to reason that a man cannot work with metal and upon metal, and finger glass and metal and wear no gloves and not leave his finger prints.[140]

Next, the attorneys attacked the testimony of the streetcar conductor.

The conductor who said that Joe Weaver left the Square on the Madison street car, westbound at 9:05 on cross-examination admitted that he was given this time by the police; that he could not tell at what hour he had left any other time that night at the Square, although he had made six round trips that night. He admitted that the police suggested to him that a tall Negro was the man who committed the murder, and he further admitted that when he was taken to the Central station to identify this man who boarded the car, the Defendant was the only tall Negro who was placed behind the screen. This man could not describe any other person who rode his street car that night.

As to the conductor who said Joe Weaver boarded his street car at West 105th Street and Madison Avenue on Sunday night… at 10:30…this man says his car arrived and picked up five passengers at 105th Street and Madison Avenue at 10:30, that it could not have been as early as 10:25, nor could it have been as late as 10:35; that he was positive it was exactly 10:30….

It is to be remembered that the American District Telegraph Company's representative testified that at 10:30… the watchman rang in from box number 17. We know that the American District Telegraph Company's system of ringing in of watchmen is correct to the minute. The undisputed testimony in this case is that the man was murdered 100 feet from box number 17. From where the man was murdered to where Alex Maynor left part of his coat when going over the fence was quite a distance. And from this fence or gate, where the piece of coat was left on the barbed wire, to the place where the conductor said the Defendant boarded his street car, the conductor says is at least 200 feet. Therefore the Defendant could not have committed the crime upon the watchman who was at box 17 at 10:30, and who walked 100 feet before being shot.

Can it be said that the conductors of the Cleveland Railway Company in any respect corroborated the testimony of Alex Maynor?

The testimonies of the two conductors were weighed against those of Joe's landlady, his room mate, and Mrs. Cook who had said when she went to bed Joe Weaver was still in the house. And there were the testimonies of other corroborating defense witnesses: Jesse Levy, Dan Hall, Fannie Siler, Nettie Pope, George and Hattie Johnson.

All the above witnesses placed Joe Weaver from 7:30 p.m. until after 10:00 p.m. on Sunday night, March 13th, between East 37th and East 57th Streets, which is from fifty minutes to an hour's distance from the scene of the crime by street car, and from twenty to twenty-five minutes by street car from the Square where the conductor said he boarded the car at 9:05....

The State failed to make a case against Weaver by even a preponderance of the evidence, much less by establishing the guilt of the accused beyond a reasonable doubt.

We therefore respectfully submit to this honorable Court that there is no evidence in this case of sufficient substance to come within the rules of Criminal Law with respect to reasonable doubt, and that Your Honor will not permit a man to be sent to the electric chair upon the sole testimony of a confessed burglar and murderer who said that the Defendant was with him on that night.

It is plain enough to see why Alex Maynor wanted to put it on someone else and why he picked out Joe Weaver: Because he had Joe Weaver's gun.

Can any Court give credence to the testimony of an accomplice when he says that he went to the place to commit burglary and did not expect to get any of the loot or spoil? And the only reason he can give for going out to commit a burglary was because the other man "suaded" him?

We respectfully request on behalf of a poor Georgia Negro boy whose record in the past has been flawless that this Court grant him the privilege of having a second jury pass upon the facts in this case before he be electrocuted.

We as attorney for this indigent prisoner sincerely hope that we are not stepping beyond the rules of ethics of our profession when we state to the Court that we personally believe Joe Weaver to be innocent of this crime, and personally pray to this Court to grant him a new trial. This appeal is made not in our professional capacity, but as citizens of Ohio, wishing to see justice done and cringing at the idea of an innocent man being electrocuted.[141]

The idleness of prison life soon began to weigh heavily upon the man once respected in his community as a hard worker. Joe thought he would "go crazy" confined to his cell 23 hours a day with nothing to do but to listen to condemned men plot their escape, curse the night, all while clinging to hope for favor from the Governor. Men so desperate some set fire to their cots, trying to escape the chair.

Of them Weaver [said later], "It isn't prison that makes you tough, but the inmates. Man, man, they sho' are hard-boiled."[142]

After a while Joe noticed that many of the men could neither read nor write. He "sorta" became their secretary.

Days no longer idle, he became one of the most useful men within the walls. He read the Bible to the men, encouraged them to sing spirituals, taught some of the more illiterate prisoners to read and write, cheered the despondent men who sat in the

gloomy cages, and fanned the spark of optimism that lay at the
bottom of their unhappy souls.[143]

"No, no! Not 'moosic.' Meusic," Joe said to his student who
was foreign-born. Next thing that young man knew, he was
crooning spirituals.

The Hungarian youth had arrived at the penitentiary two
weeks ahead of Weaver and was put in a cell with colored men.
Fistfights that broke out repeatedly along racial lines prompted
the young man to ask to be put into a cell with "someone (he)
could get along with."

That someone turned out to be another "colored" man.

Along with the secretarial and mentoring tasks to keep him
busy, Joe had the responsibility of special watch over John
Bradshaw, said to be one of the most unmanageable prisoners
ever to enter the penitentiary. In time, John succumbed to Joe
Weaver's spiritual influence, but first he had to come to respecting
Joe's strength.

To get through all this, three times a day and at midnight, Joe
knelt and prayed some variation of: "Lord, you know I'm innocent.
Make it known and fight my battle."[144]

All through this trying period, the death row inmate pleaded
for a chance to talk to Alex Mayner, but the warden would not
allow the conversation to take place, fearing violence.

When Joe first arrived on death row, George Vargo from Lake
County was already in the cell. Vargo's lawyers had won a new
trial for him in 1926, but not a reversal of his sentence. He told
Joe that he had put away his wife because she wouldn't cook corned
beef and cabbage for him.

John Hickman and Leo Halterman were put in the death cell
block about a month after Joe's arrival. Hickman had been
convicted of killing a policeman; Halterman of killing both his
brother and his sister-in-law. Vargo and Halterman were executed
on June 10th, Hickman a week later.

Phil Orleck was under sentence of death for killing a guard in
the Mansfield Reformatory. Many nights the despondent Orleck
came to the Joe for words of scripture and prayer—or simply to

be cheered up by a man whose own death by electrocution was nearing. Had Orleck been executed as scheduled, June 10th would have seen a triple execution. Instead, he was put to death 38 days later.

Whenever a man walked past him for the last time, Joe would lie back on his cot and his imagination would take over: What was it like at the end of that walk?

The black door opens to admit the chaplain into the death chamber. His steps are deliberate, his mood solemn. His lips utter scripture. The prisoner trails him in, the doomed man's legs draining of blood demanded by his heart. A pair of guards bring up the rear, steady in their walk.

Pictures ring the room—the grim faces of predecessors, the first one in 1897 when electrocution became the state's preferred method of execution. There's space on the wall to post one more face—his. A mere step up and he is on the platform. Two officers position him between the outstretched arms and into the welcoming lap of a Frankenstein-like monster.

A spot the size of a quarter has been shaven from the top of the man's head. One of the guards straps in his ankles, knees, arms, and shoulders. Another dampens the exposed calf of his right leg with a solution of salamoniac and water.

The negative electrode is attached to his leg, the positive one to his scalp. The bare spot is dampened by a guard to facilitate the drive of the current to his brain. Everything has been checked and is in working order. Everything is ready.

An uneasy quiet settles over the chamber and the cell block beyond. The Death Angel slinks in. Sensing its presence, the attending guards back away, having lowered the hood over the man's eyes.

"Have you anything to say?" the warden asks.

Regardless, he signals finally. A circuit connects in the control room. The two electrodes send current back and forth. The light above the chair changes from blue to red. The man's body strains against the straps. The hum of electricity fills the ears of witnesses, two of whom are newsmen, one from the state capital, and the other from the dying man's hometown. His brain sizzles, his muscles swell almost to the bursting point. Nineteen hundred and fifty volts for 10 seconds. The body stiffens. Another 500 volts for 40 seconds more. A puff of smoke emits from the exposed right calf. Ten seconds again at 1,950 volts to ensure heart stoppage.

Satiated, the Angel leaves—not unaccompanied. Prison physicians step forward and pronounce the remains dead.[145]

Two days before his August 12th electrocution date, Joe noted in the diary that he kept throughout his incarceration: How awful it is to die in cold blood, counting the day and hours, and even the minutes.[146]

The execution was postponed until October 12th.

Joe fervently prayed his legal team would prevail in their feverish effort to get the jury's decision reversed. In a feature article in the *Plain Dealer*, Regine V. Kurlander said later:

> He had been framed, they were certain, by those too eager to collect the reward of $1,000. Maynor's testimony that Weaver had been his accomplice and the one to fire the shot seemed thin against Weaver's simplicity and adherence to his original story, denying any part in the robbery and the subsequent killing.
>
> He was singularly fortunate that Marsteller was on the case, for this attorney is a southerner and understands Weaver as a northerner could scarcely hope to do. An affection sprang up between them, not uncommon to the two races who dwell side by side and yet fundamentally are miles apart.[147]

Seven days before his October appointment, Joe Weaver received another stay of execution, this time until November 15th. Two days before the November date, Cook and Marsteller visited him in his cell with news of another month's postponement. That gained them time to file a motion for a hearing before the state supreme court.

"Are you feeling nervous?" Cook asked.

"Oh, not very. I knew if you didn't come here today, you'd come in tomorrow, and if you didn't come in tomorrow, you'd come the next day. And when you came, I knew you'd bring good news."[148]

The amazed look on Cook's face caused his client to laugh. So infectious was the laughter, Cook could only join in.

"You've guessed it right. We've got another stay. But I expected to find you awfully down in the mouth, with one or two days to go before you were to die."

Joe said nothing more, not wanting to let on how he really felt—afraid that this time was the last.[149]

Once, when Joe was within two days of execution, Cook showed up again to tell his client of another stay.

> "Are you surprised, Joe?" [he asked.]
> "No, suh," replied Joe. "I knew you was comin'. I've been sayin' to the Lord: 'Lord, Lord, you won't turn your child down.' Since I know I'm his child, I'll hold him to his word."[150]

CHAPTER 9

CONVICTION IN CUYAHOGA COUNTY

In the waning hours of January 6, 1928, prisoner number 57114 was put to death, at age 17—the youngest person the state of Ohio had ever executed. [In Joe Weaver's view, Floyd Hewitt had not the mind of a 7-year-old and did not realize what he was doing when] he beat to death a young Conneaut woman and her five-year-old child. Just before the execution, Floyd's aged father came to the death cell and stood in a pool of tears. Unmoved when his aggrieved father was led away, Floyd turned to his condemned fellows and laughed, and was laughing when his name was called for the march into eternity.[151]

Early in January 1928, Judge Carpenter made a trip down state. He spent a day at the penitentiary questioning Alex Mayner to satisfy him that the testimony he had heard from this man was the truth. The sentencing judge talked with Mayner and other prisoners. He left convinced, he said, that the state's key testifier had in fact told the truth, a conclusion he put in a letter to the prosecutor.[152]

Warden Thomas sent for Alex Mayner and told the state's chief witness to go back to his cell, "get down on his knees and pray."

107

Alex said he believed in hell, after which the warden told him there wouldn't be a corner there hot enough to hold him if he let Weaver go to the chair knowing him to be innocent.[153]

With their client's January 20th electrocution looming, Cook and Marsteller made a direct plea to the Governor. They characterized Alex Mayner as a schemer whose aim was to place the fatal gun in someone else's hand, someone not present at the time of the slaying.

> The undersigned have had two conferences with Chaplain Thomas O. Reed, and he has expressed to us that Weaver is innocent. Upon our last personal interview with the Chaplain, he informed us that Alex Maynor admitted to him that he had a gun in his possession on the night of the murder.[154]

Alex having denied that on the witness stand, the chaplain had promised to do whatever he could to get the truth out of Alex by Friday, January 6th, the Plaintiffs told the Governor, but they feared he might not have an opportunity to do so before January 20th.

The letter to Governor A. Vic Donahey said further that the undersigned (William F. Marsteller and Nathan E. Cook) had started their own independent investigation after the guilty verdict came in. This done entirely at their own expense, including the cost of appeal.

> ...We made a thorough investigation through attorneys in his home state and found Joe Weaver had never violated any law or been arrested or implicated in any crime or misdemeanor. His record is absolutely clean, and shows that he was a hard worker, a steady worker, made good wages, and besides that, attended night schools so that he might learn to read and write correctly. His Army record was perfect and he received an honorable discharge.
> The undersigned are in no way interested in Weaver personally, further than to see that justice is done. It is not our intention to invoke the aid of so-called uplifting societies, nor is it our intention

to attempt to bring political or other pressure to bear upon you to save the life of the man we believe to be innocent.

We do, however, want you to know that in our opinion, after having spent nine months in painstaking and thorough investigation, and having received dozens of letters from Weaver, which in our opinion could not have been written by a guilty man, we still believe in his innocence.

We believe that the jury found their verdict through passion and prejudice and that the State of Ohio will snuff out the life of an innocent man if you permit Joseph Weaver to be electrocuted.

It is our opinion that no harm will come to the State of Ohio if the sentence of Joseph Weaver is commuted to life imprisonment, because we feel that there is not the slightest doubt in the world that some day Alex Maynor will tell the truth about what happened at Midland Steel Products Company on March 13th, and Joseph Weaver will be freed from the penitentiary, return to his proper place in society and the record of the State of Ohio for fairness, justice and equality will not have been besmirched by the taking of the life of an innocent man.[155]

Meanwhile, the judge's inquiries at the prison stirred the interest of Chaplain Reed. Not long after that visit, the chaplain was a dinner guest in Warden Preston E. Thomas's penitentiary quarters. Reed honored the promise he had made by asking the warden to allow him to bring together the two men convicted of killing Jasper Russell. With permission, he set up a meeting for January 12th.

On that day, Reed took inmate No. 57028 to the part of the prison reserved for condemned men, at which time the chaplain said to Alex Mayner, "If Weaver is innocent, for God's sake, say so."

In the death row section of the old limestone cell block the chaplain and the lifer talked for about an hour with Joe Weaver. On the way back to his part of the prison, Mayner broke down. He had lied, he told Reed. On the witness stand, under oath he had lied. And now he was sorry. Another man had done the killing.

Chaplain Reed hurried his charge to the warden's office for a retelling of the confession in front of the prison head. Joe Weaver was brought in to hear the man—once a friend, co-worker, and customer—say, "he didn't know a blessed thing about it."[156]

"Why did you do this thing to me, Alex? Ain't I been good to you? When you stayed at my house, I covered you up at night with my blanket. Why did you do this to me?"[157]

Mayner said he thought it would be easy to hang the crime on Weaver.

When Prosecutor Stanton learned that Mayner had changed his story, he said a full investigation would be made, and sent out two detective lieutenants to find the man Alex had named as the trigger man. Word of the recantation quickly reached the state house, whereupon the chief executive declared Ohio would not electrocute an innocent man so long as he was governor. Members of the board of clemency were called, their job being to hear Alex's full statement.[158]

The matter would be taken up immediately, a board spokesman said, and if the new evidence satisfied them, they would recommend to the Governor yet another stay. Cook and Marsteller had been rushing around frantically since the supreme court turned down their application for a rehearing of the case. They announced their intention to go before the state supreme court and demand a stay.

Judge Carpenter made it clear that he would look favorably upon a plea for a new trial.

"I had serious doubts, for it was simply a case of one man's word against another's," he said.[159]

Alex claimed he could not recall the name of the man who had actually done the killing. Later he offered the name Frank Jones.

Warden Thomas was a doubter of Jones's existence.

"Now is the time when one of those lie detecting machines would come in good use to settle the question of Maynor's truthfulness," he said.[160]

CHAPTER 10

CONFESSION IN COLUMBUS

The hearing before the Board of Clemency began at the prison on Monday morning, January 16, 1928. Dan W. Williams and George A. Edge were members of the board, F. O. Howell, the board's secretary. The governor's office was represented by C. H. Sisson. Chaplain Thomas O. Reed was on hand, as was Cuyahoga County Prosecutor Edward Stanton. Nathan Cook and William Marsteller were present as the attorneys for the Plaintiff against the Defendant, the State of Ohio. And, of course, at the center of the hearing was Alex Mayner.

Dan Williams led off the questioning for the state.

"What is your name?"

"Mayner."

"How do you spell it?"

"A-l-e-x M-a-y-n-e-r. Since I have been here, they put an 'o' in it. My name is Mayner. 'O' don't belong there."

"What is your sentence here?"

"With life."

"What is it for?"

"Well, it is on this crime they got—Jasper Russell crime."

"Did you plead guilty?"

"Yes sir, I pleaded guilty, if you understand—"

"I will ask you another question. Are you guilty?"

"No sir," [Mayner replied.]

"What is the name of the man that was killed?"

"Jasper Russell, and so I want to speak to Mr. Reed here just a minute. This morning I told him the whole history and I told him some things which I ain't never sir, told, you understand—"

"That you did not tell me," [Chaplain Reed interjected.]

"Yes sir. So he told me to come with the clean thing."

"That is the thing to do," [the chaplain said.]

"I told him since I had a talk with him, I felt more better, you understand, and so I told him if you all would allow me a few minutes—"

"I will ask you the questions I want you to answer," [said Williams.]

"All right sir."

"Did you see this man killed?"

"No sir, no sir."

"Were you there where he was killed?"

[Alex denied being present.]

"How far away were you?"

"I was at home."

"I said, 'How far away were you?' Tell me that."

"Why, the job that was done, it is about six or seven miles, I reckon, as near as I can get at—maybe further than that, for all I know."

[The state's key witness now said he did not know who killed Jasper Russell.]

"I will ask you that again. Do you know who killed this man?"

"No sir. And the reason—"

"Wait, now. Did anyone tell you who killed this man?"

"No sir."

"Well, now, that is all about that. I am going to ask you about something else."

[Alex was asked about his testimony in the Jasper Russell case.]

"Did you tell the court and the jury who killed this man?"

"Yes sir. Yes sir."

"You told a lie then to me a little while ago?"

"How is that? I know I told you—"

"Wait. You told a lie to me a little while ago," [said Williams.]

"I told you I didn't know who killed him."

"Did you tell the court who did it?"

"Yes sir, but you see—"

"You told the court you knew who did it?"

"Yes sir."

"Did you lie to the court?"

"Yes sir, and if you let—"

"Wait, now. Now I will ask you that again. I don't want you to be a liar unless you want to be. Did you lie when you testified in the court?"

"Yes sir, I did. Yes sir, I did," [said Joe's accuser.]

"Did you lie about yourself?"

"Yes sir."

"Did you lie about anyone else?"

"Yes sir."

"About how many people did you lie?"

"How many did I lie?"

"Lie about, yes."

"Lie about," [echoed Mayner.] "I lied about Weaver and I lied about this other man that I told you."

"Frank Jones," [said Chaplain Reed.]

"Yes sir. And myself is three."

"You mention a Jones, do you?" [asked Williams.]

"Yes sir."

[Asked by the board member whether he knew Jones and Joe Weaver, Alex replied that he did not know Jones, but he did know Joe Weaver.]

"How long have you known Weaver?"

"How long I been knowing Weaver? I guess about three or four years, as near as I can get at it."

"Know him well?"

"Yes sir, know him pretty well. He know me perfectly well."

"When was Bell [sic] killed?"

"When was Bell killed? I don't know when he was killed."

113

"Don't know anything about it?"

"No sir."

"Were you with Weaver when Bell was killed?" [asked Williams.]

"No sir."

"Were you with Weaver when Russell was killed?"

"No sir, no sir."

"You weren't with him?"

"No sir."

"Do you know where he was then?"

"Where Joe was?"

"Weaver?"

"No sir."

"You don't know where he was?"

"No sir."

"Did you tell the court you knew where he was?"

"Yes sir."

"You lied, then?"

"Yes sir. I lied there then on Weaver. Now you understand—"

"Did you tell the court Weaver was with you?" [Williams asked, interrupting Mayner].

"Yes sir. And I told you Jones, then I lied on him."

"Why did you pick on Weaver at the time, and say he was the man with you?" [board member George Edge asked.]

"Well, if you all just give me a chance, I will tell you all. When they come and arrest me, you understand, my wife was sick and she was seriously sick. They asked me, I says, 'why' when they arrested me and they asked me where I did go Sunday. I says I was home all day Sunday and I says my wife come back from Reverend Giller's [sic—Ailer's] church, that is between 37th and— between Woodland and Scope [sic—Scovill]," [said Mayner.] "I says after she come back from church, I says, Mr. Martin, the same man that was trying to make me say he was in, I says, 'We drove over to this white man's house, me and him worked together every day.' I says when they arrested me, the officer come and says, 'Mayner, do you live here?' and I told him yes. He says, 'Is you a piano player?' I says, 'No.' He says, 'Well, we know good and damn well that you lied, that you know something about it.'

114

He says, 'Now, you might as well tell us the truth, we done got the man that done it,' you understand, and I says, 'No,' and he says, 'Well, would you mind come and go down with us?' Well, I goes on down with them."

"Who did you tell this to?" [asked Edge.]

"To the officer."

"When they came to arrest you?"

"Yes sir, and so they brung me on down. Well, they put me into a room, knocked out some of my teeth, broke out some ribs, stamped me and kicked me."

"Where are these teeth that were knocked out?" [Dan Williams asked.]

"One here and one here and got some loose here. You can take your finger—"

"How many knocked out?"

"One."

"Who knocked it out?"

"The officer."

"What is the name of the officer?"

"Well, I don't know the name now, to tell you the truth."

"You want to be careful about that. You are lying again?"

"No, I ain't."

"Hold on," [Williams said.] "You have done so much lying, it is pretty hard to believe you. Be careful before you say anybody knocked your teeth out."

"They did."

"What is his name?"

"The first man that come and arrested me. He is the tall old man."

"Just drop that tooth business, and tell Mr. Edge what he asked you," Williams said.

"The principal thing I want is just why you said Weaver was with you, without any circumlocution," [said George Edge].

"After they got me down there, understand, they takes me over, understand, after they beat me and carried it on out and says, 'What guy's name you got on a piece of paper?' I told them Joseph Weaver, and they says, 'He must have been with you, wasn't he?' I says, 'No,' and they tuned in and hit me again, see. They beat me up there, went on out the room and brung my wife in and she is a large fat woman and suffering with heart trouble," [Mayner explained.] "She come in crying and they says, 'Well, God damn you, if you don't tell something, we will hold this woman here, just on account of your God damn lying,' and says, 'The quicker you tell us, the quicker we will quit beating you and let her go home,' and they had her in the Central Police Station and they done take my children and carried them out to the 'tention home, they call it, something like that. He held my wife from that night until—they arrested me on Monday—until the next day about 11:00 before they would turn here [sic] loose and she was so sick and nervous and she come down the next two days and seen me, see, and then after I told them who it was, they quit this beating then, brung me on back into the cell and says, 'Now you can go and wash your face and lay down.' I went and washed my face and laid down. I was in there about a half hour and so he come, the officer come again, he says, 'Mayner', I says, 'All right.' He says, 'You know what kind of a God damn lie you told?' I says, 'What is that?' He says, he told me—and this ain't never been mentioned up at any Court House—"

"Answer Mr. Edge's question. Don't tell what this other fellow said," [Williams said.]

"I want to give him an idea of it, you understand."

"You said you gave his name because you had it on a slip in your pocket. How did it happen to be there?" [Williams asked.]

"How did it come me having it? I had done seen him about ordering some cloth to make my wife a suit and he give me his address. That is what I was doing with it and they asked me and made me lie on myself and I didn't know what in the name of the Lord to do. I told the Father when I come over here, I says, 'I am going to tell the truth or die, yes sir. Jesus in Heaven this morning, he had a great blame to bear and there it is, and still he pulled it through.'"

"What I asked you awhile ago," [said Williams.] "You still stick to it? You told a lie to the court against Weaver?"

"Yes sir."

"You were under oath when you told that?"

"Yes sir, under oath.""Yes.""Yes sir."

"You swore to that?"

"Yes sir."

"Did you swear to any statements you made afterwards?"

"Afterwards, here," [said Mayner.] "No more than what I told Chaplain Reed and the Warden, understand."

"When you were in the court, you held up your hand like this?"

"Yes sir."

"And swore to tell the truth?"

[Alex affirmed that he had sworn to tell the truth, the whole truth, and nothing but the truth.]

"Then you sat down in a chair?"

"Yes sir."

"Then they asked you questions."

"Yes sir."

"Do you know Mr. Stanton?" [Williams asked.]

"Yes sir, this is him over there."

"That is the man over there?"

"Yes sir. I knowed him as soon as I walked in here, I knew him."

"Just a minute. Did Mr. Stanton hit you over the head and knock your teeth out—that man there?"

"No sir," [Mayner replied.]

"No threats from Mr. Stanton?"

"No sir, that man there?"

"Yes."

"No sir."

"Knock any teeth out?"

"No sir."

"Threaten you?"

"No sir."

"Or anyone else?"

"No sir."

"I mean when you were on the chair?"

"No sir."

"Nobody threatened you," [Williams asked again.]

"No sir."

"Was the Judge looking at you?"

"No sir."

"Did he threaten you?"

"No sir."

"Nobody threatened you?"

"No, sir."

"Why did you lie?"

"Well, the way—"

"Hold on. Why did you lie?" [Williams asked, interrupting.]

"Well, the condition, you understand, what my lawyer, he was there, understand, told me what he was trying to do for me."

"Did your lawyer ask you to say Weaver did it?"

"No sir, he never did. And I have lied to him and I lied in court. So I am coming this morning with the clean truth. Whether you all believe me or not, I can't help. But it is true from Heaven."

[The reins of interrogation were taken over by George Edge.]

"You had a trial; you did not plead guilty?"

"What say?"

"You plead [*sic*] guilty?"

"Yes."

[Alex was asked whether he had pled guilty to the shooting, or to the robbery, or to both.]

"I just plead guilty about being out there, you understand, but I wasn't there, you understand; you understand me, don't you?"

"I understand your statement now," [said Edge.] "What company was it that this man was the watchman for?"

"For the Midland Products."

"Did you ever work there?"

"Yes sir."

"You had worked there?"

"Working there every day."

"Weaver had worked there too?"

"Yes sir."

"Did they owe him some money?"

"Yes sir."

"Did they owe him some money, wages?"

"I heard they owed him some, yes."

"Where did you hear that?"

118

"He told it," [Mayner replied.]

"When?" [asked Edge.]

"Sir?"

"At what time did he tell you that?"

"Oh, I don't know what time it was when he told me, nothing like that, you understand."

"A week or two weeks before the time of this murder?"

"Well, it might have been about a week, I reckon."

"How long had he been away from there?"

"Well, how long—"

"How long before the murder when he had quit work?"

"I do not know; I don't know how long it was, you see," [said Mayner.] "And I didn't know that he was away from there for a long time, and the reason I knowed he was away from there then there was a press I used to work at, his foreman come over there and seen my foreman and got me to come over there and worked until he got some man over there to take that frame job, automobile frame job, you understand."

"So you are telling the truth what you are telling this morning?" [asked Edge.]

"Yes sir."

[Board member Williams interjected a question.]

"How much of that is the truth?"

"I say I come here to tell the truth if I fall dead."

"How much of it is true?"

"Every bit of it," [Mayner declared.]

[Nathan Cook spoke up.]

"May we have the privilege of questioning the man, please, we as attorneys, Mr. Marsteller and myself, as attorneys for Joseph Weaver, the man who is vitally interest in the matter, sentenced to be electrocuted on Friday night of this week?"

"Mr. Chaplain, the warden is not able to be here," [Williams asked.]

"No, he and Mr. Harper had a conference, Mr. Williams."

"Do you know what the warden's rule is about matters of this kind?"

"No, I don't, Mr. Williams, I couldn't say. I couldn't say one way or the other."

"You know this man is the warden's prisoner."

"There is a question or two I would like to ask him," [Chaplain Reed said.]

[Williams said it was the chaplain's right to question the prisoner, so Reed asked Alex if he knew how much money Weaver earned at the plant.]

"Weaver made all the way around some days $8.50, $9.00, $15.00 a day."

"Another question I want to ask you," [said Reed.] "In going over the fence, some fellow in going over the fence tore his coat and they claimed that was your overcoat, didn't they?"

"Yes."

"That piece matched with your coat."

"The way they cut the pieces out of my coat."

"They claimed it was a piece of your overcoat?"

"Yes sir, and the men that was working there had the same make overcoat I had, the same material, cloth and all."

"Well, now listen, Mayner. When you came and made this confession to me, you said Weaver wasn't there, didn't you?"

"Yes sir."

"That you was there?"

"Yes sir."

"Mr. Williams and Mr. Edge," [Chaplain Reed said.] "I don't know whether you got that last question; I would like you to hear this; the man that went over the fence, whoever committed this crime had on an overcoat and the overcoat was torn by the barbed wire and a piece was left there; this piece tallied with the overcoat, in the torn place, that Mayner wore that night, isn't that a fact?"

"Yes, but still when I seen my overcoat, it was a round hole cut out of my coat."

"The record says that the piece fit in the place torn in your coat—the same length, the same color and all; that is a fact?"

"Yes sir."

"You sit here and tell this clemency board you weren't there," [the chaplain asked.]

"Yes sir."

"Last week you told me you were there?"

"Yes."

"And that another man was with you?"

"Yes sir," [Mayner answered.]

"And you tell this body of men, this board, that Joseph Weaver wasn't there?"

"Yes."

"That it was Frank Jones?"

"Yes."

"What did I tell you when I took you over to interview Weaver?"

"Interview Weaver."

"What did I tell you about the guilty party," [the chaplain asked.] "Tell this board; did I say to you that if Weaver is the guilty man, say so?"

"Yes sir, you did."

"If he is not, say no?"

"Yes sir, you did, actually you did."

[Dan Williams resumed his interrogation and pressed more deeply into that part of Mayner's testimony.]

"You said Weaver was the guilty man to the court, didn't you?"

"Yes sir."

"Do you know that Weaver is not the guilty man?"

"Yes sir."

"How?"

"Well, I wasn't with him, you understand."

"How do you know he is not the guilty man?"

"If he ain't the guilty man, I do not know now—"

"Hold on, now," [said Williams.] "How do you know he is not the guilty man?"

"Well, I wasn't with him."

"You don't know, do you?"

"No, I wasn't with him,"

"You think that over, now, if you want to say anything else; how do you know that Weaver did not kill him?"

"Well, I do not know in one way."

"You don't know?"

"No," [Mayner replied.]

[Hence, the state's key witness—the one who had sworn during the trial that Joe Weaver shot and killed Jasper Russell—could neither confirm nor deny the convicted man's guilt because Mayner was not with him.]

[It was again Chaplain Reed's turn to interrogate.]

"Do you know a man inside by the name of Murphy?"

"Murphy?"

"Works in the same construction gan [sic] with you."

"No sir, I don't."

"Do you ever remember making a remark in there to two or three fellows when you were talking about the electric chair, and you said, 'Well, there is one fellow I sent to the chair'?"

"I never used that word any way, shape, form or talks. You know I have had more to say to you and the Warden—"

"How does it come and you come and make this confession to me that you were there and Weaver was [not] there and name a man with you and, in the presence of Warden Thomas say you can't remember the other fellow's name, and go to Father O'Brien this morning and say, 'I want to tell the truth'?"

"He sent for me," [Mayner replied.]

"He had a right to do that; you told Father O'Brien you weren't there, how does it come then you told Judge Carpenter and Warden Thomas that Weaver is absolutely the man; how can this board and these ladies who have come here know you are telling the truth this morning?"

"I actually is telling the truth."

"You told me that the other day?"

"Yes."

"You told Judge Carpenter you were telling the truth," [the chaplain said. Presumably, this is when Judge Carpenter visited the prison and talked with Mayner.]

"The circumstances I was in and misery, I say to that gentleman over there, the way I was whipped, beat me—"

"You haven't been whipped since you were here?"

"No."

"You have lied to the Warden, to Judge Carpenter and to me and evidently you lied to Father O'Brien somewhere."

"I have told all the truth."

"We can't be sure, because you have told three different stories."

"I have told the truth."

"Three different stories," [Reed said.] "That is all I want to ask."

[The interrogation was volleyed again to board member Williams.]

"Now, what you have said to Mr. Edge over here, this gentleman, and to me, you knew that you did not have to answer the questions, did you not?"

"Did I know?"

"You knew that you did not have to answer any questions?"

"Did I know I didn't have to answer none?"

"We did not force you to answer?"

"No, no, you didn't," [Mayner said.]

"Everything you have said, you were willing to say, were you not?"

"Yes. You all didn't force me to say it or nothing like that. You didn't offer to hit me or nothing at all."

"You don't have to answer, except what you want to say. I am going to ask you again," [said Williams.] "Did you kill this man?"

"No sir."

"Do you know who killed him?"

[Alex said he did not know who had killed Jasper Russell.]

"Did you say that Weaver did kill him?"

"Yes sir."

"Did you lie when you said that?"

"Yes sir."

"Do you see anybody here that you know in this room?"

"That gentleman there, this man here and these three right here. And I have seen that one there, and I seen this one here the other day I think, if I don't make a mistake, I ain't sure, but these here I seen the other day."

"Do you know that Weaver did not kill this man?"

"I do not know."

[Williams pointed first to Nathan Cook and then to William Marsteller. He asked Alex whether he had seen them, respectively, in court. Alex said he had. Williams told Alex that the two men were attorneys and that they had asked to question him.]

"Are you perfectly willing to answer them?"

"Well, if I can I will answer them."

[Board member Williams asked the chaplain whether he thought the warden would have any objections. Reed said he didn't think so. Howell, the board's secretary, agreed.]

"We want to get to the fact," [Reed said.]

"We are familiar with the record, both Mr. Cook and myself," [Bill Marsteller said.] "This is Mr. Cook of Cleveland."

[The second attorney for the Plaintiff began the counter-questioning.]

"Alex," [said Nate Cook,] "you remember that I am the man who cross-examined you when you were on the witness stand in Cleveland last April?"

"Yes sir."

"You testified for the State of Ohio against Joseph Weaver?"

"Yes sir."

[Cook gave a summary of the first degree murder charge against the Plaintiff and how Jasper Russell had been shot at the steel plant.]

"Yes, but I wasn't there," [said Mayner.]

"But you testified that you were there?"

"Yes."

"You testified that Joseph Weaver was with you there, didn't you?"

"Yes."

"Tell us now as you would answer to your God, Alex," [said Cook.] "Was or was not Joseph Weaver at that plant with you that night?"

"No sir, neither one of us."

[Note: There are only two ways Mayner could know that Joe Weaver was not there at the time of the murder. Either Mayner was elsewhere with Joe, or Mayner was present when the murder occurred and knew that Joe was not with him. If Mayner was not at Midland Steel that night, as he said, he could not speak of whether Joe was at the plant or not. Apparently, Mayner was trying to get himself off the hook, and at the same time, declare that he was not in a position to point the finger of guilt at Joe Weaver.]

"And when you told Judge Carpenter and that jury in that courtroom in the presence of Mr. Marsteller and myself and

Prosecutor Stanton and his assistant, Mr. Connell, that Joseph Weaver was there, you lied."

"Yes."

"And you are now telling the truth, as you hope to face your Maker," [said Cook.] "Is that true?"

"Yes sir. Yes sir."

"On the witness stand you testified, Alex, did you not, that you saw Joseph Weaver about noon time at your house?"

"Yes sir."

"He came there for the purpose of seeing whether or not you wanted a piece of cloth for a new dress for your wife, isn't that so?"

"Yes."

"He told you at that time that he had changed his address?"

"Yes."

"And that when you wanted that new piece of cloth, you could get him at his new address, isn't that so?"

"That is right."

"In order for you to have that new address he rote [*sic*] his address one night, his name and his address only, on East 59th Street on a slip of paper?"

"Yes."

"And you put that slip of paper in your pocket."

"Yes," [said Mayner.]

"That was after your wife went to church that night?"

"Yes."

"And that address that he wrote on the slip of paper was on East 59th Street near East Central Avenue, wasn't it?"

"Yes."

"And that was the place where Joseph Weaver lived with a woman named Evelyn Bedell?"

"The people, I don't know the name. I ain't never seen her or been to her house."

"You weren't in the court room when Mrs. Bedell testified," [asked Cook.] "You were in the court just for a few minutes?"

"Yes."

"After Joseph Weaver left you on Sunday, you met a man named B. Martin, didn't you?"

"Yes."

"Is B. Martin a colored boy or a white man?"

"You can't hardly tell him from a white man. He is about this man's height."

"He is colored?"

"Yes."

"How tall is he?"

"About that man's height over there, but heavy."

"His wife was with him, wasn't she?"

"Yes."

"And yours with you—is your testimony on the witness stand—you and your wife and B. Martin and his wife went to a gypsy's house?"

"Yes."

"What was your testimony about what you did over there?"

"We went over there to get wine and set down and drink," [said Mayner.]

"Were you there very long?" [Nate Cook asked.] "Didn't you testify you were there from half past seven or eight to four in the afternoon?"

"Yes."

"And you, among the four of you, consumed a couple of gallons of wine, didn't you that afternoon?"

"Yes."

"And then you went to your house didn't you on East 40th Street."

"Yes."

"Your wife was sick then, wasn't she?"

"Yes."

"When did you next see Joseph Weaver?"

"Well, when I next saw Joseph Weaver, that is when they had me and him in the Central Police Station."

"Then, when you testified that he came to your house at nine o'clock that night to get you to go to the Midland Steel Products Company, you lied, didn't you?"

"Yes."

"You wouldn't see Joseph Weaver again after noon that day," [said Cook.] "Did you?"

"No."

"The first time you ever saw him after that was in Central Police Station after you had been arrested?"

"Yes, Central Police Station."

[Cook then asked Mayner about a stepson. Mayner confirmed that he had one.]

"What is his name?"

"Joe Haines."

"How big is Joe?"

"Him and Joe Weaver are about the same height and complexion and all."

"Same height and complexion and all," [Cook said.]

"Yes."

"And one could easily be mistaken for the other."

"Yes," [Mayner replied.]

"A street car conductor who happened to see them get on a car couldn't tell the difference?"

"No."

"Has Joe Haines any fingers off?"

"No."

"Is there anything the matter with either one of his hands?"

"Not as I know of, now. Of course since I have been down here, may be something the matter with one hand."

"But nothing the matter with his hands when you saw him last?"

"No."

"When did you see him last, see Joe Haines last?"

"When did I seen Joe Haines last? It was a Saturday, some officer come and got me right from the jail and after we come out of the jail we come back this way where them automobiles are parked and went into the office."

"Did you ever see Joe Haines just before you were arrested?" [Cook asked.]

"No."

"How long before you were arrested was the last time you saw Joe Haines?"

"Well, from the last time I seen him, that is when I got the end of that finger there cut off."

"When was that?"

127

"That was just over a year ago until he come down there to the jail to see me and brung me some cigarettes to smoke and chewing tobacco."

"That was the last time you ever saw him after the murder was committed?"

"Yes."

"Did you ever have a gun in your possession?" [Nate Cook asked.]

"No."

"Never did have any, [at] any time?"

"No."

"No kind of gun at all?"

"No sir."

[Interrogation for the Plaintiff was relayed from Cook to his partner.]

"You remember when you testified and the state put a street car conductor on the stand?"

"Yes."

"And you said yes, that is the street car conductor of the car I rode on that night?"

"Yes."

"Were you telling the truth or lying?" [Bill Marsteller asked.]

"Lying."

"Who told you to say that was the street car conductor?"

"Who told me?"

"Yes."

"Didn't anyone."

"How did you know to say that was the street car conductor of the car you rode in that night?"

"They hadn't asked me could I or would I know, and I told them 'yes,' but at the same time I was lying."

"Now, when you saw that street car conductor, did you ever see him before you saw him in court?"

"Until I saw him in court? Yes, I—"

"You identified two separate car conductors, didn't you?"

"Yes, but I was lying."

"When these streetcar conductors said they saw you at 9:05 get off the car at the Square in Cleveland, were they telling the truth or lying?" [Marsteller asked.]

"They was lying."

"When the streetcar conductor said you got on his car at 106th Street, coming towards the Square, and he saw you, was he telling the truth or lying?"

"He was lying."

"Joe [sic], who sewed your coat up," [Marsteller said, confusing first names.]

"Who sewed my coat up?"

"Yes."

"I got my coat tore the time I worked two days after Weaver was off there before Christmas, and I went to the City Hall and I told the officer I got my overcoat tore about two or three days there before Christmas. I went down and they sent me out to that country club," [said Mayner.] "You know where that country club is away out there in Cleveland on that lake, I forget which country club it was. Well, I tore my coat that evening after I went upstairs to bring down two baskets of clothes to carry out to the laundry and I had to take them over to a place about as far as from here to the ball diamond, you know where that is, I had to take them that far."

"Who sent you to do that?"

"The lady I was working for out there."

"Weren't you working at the Midland Steel Products Company at that time?" [Marsteller asked.]

"Yes, but still they was taking in material and the men there was off at that time, and I just hated to lay around home. I takes upon myself and goes down to the City Hall and they sent me out there and I got two days work out there."

"Saturday, March 12th, that is the day before Jasper Russell was killed, you worked at the Midland Steel Products Company?"

"Yes."

"You worked all that week?"

"Yes."

"You worked the week before that steadily?"

"Until before Christmas time I was off a couple of days."

"You mean to say during Christmas?"

"Before."

"Before Christmas?"

"Yes."

"When you sewed it up?"

"Sewed it up before Christmas."

"When you told on that witness stand to the court and jury that you tore your coat going over that fence that night, sewed it up yourself and didn't tell you wife about it, what were you telling?" [Marsteller asked.]

"A lie."

"What were you telling a lie for?"

"Well, thought it would help me some, but it didn't."

"Why did you think it would help you out; who promised it would help you?"

"Didn't anyone tell me or anyone promise me."

"What was the reason, Alex, that caused you to make a different statement and say that Joe Weaver was not the man that killed Jasper Russell?"

"Well, what make me feel that way, when Chaplain Reed asked me would I like to go over and see Joe, see, and so after I went over and seen Joe and got to talking, you understand, then I didn't feel right down in here, and I told you that didn't I, Chaplain?"

"You told me your conscience got to whipping you," [the chaplain replied.]

"No other person talked to you in regard to your telling the truth about Joe Weaver except Chaplain Reed," [Marsteller asked.]

"That is right."

"And except the Warden and Judge Carpenter?"

"Yes sir."

"Any of the prisoners talk to you about this?"

"No."

"Any of them suggest anything to you about this?"

"No."

"Anybody threaten to whip you or beat you or stab you if you didn't say Joe Weaver was not there?" [asked Marsteller.]

"No."

"Any other person threaten you with bodily injury of any kind?"

"No sir."

"Your confession that Joe was not there was voluntary completely on your part?"

"Yes sir."

"You understand what voluntary means?"

"Yes."

"You made it because your conscience was whipping you?"

"That is right."

"And you want to tell the truth about Joe Weaver's connection with it now?"

"Yes sir."

"And you again say you lied when you said Weaver was there?" [Marsteller asked, seeking to spike the winning point.]

"Yes sir."

"That is all."

[Dan Williams had the final chance at Mayner.]

"Now, Alex, all that you said to these gentlemen is not a part of your hearing before us, you understand that?"

"Yes."

"You understand the questions I asked you?"

"Yes, I remember them."

"I asked you plain questions?"

"Yes."

"Do you know whether Weaver killed this man or not?"

"I don't."

"You do not?"

"I don't."

"Now, you say that you are not guilty of killing him yourself?"

"That is right."

"You lied when you plead guilty?"

"Yes sir, I lied."

"Remember, no use to give us what is called 'bunk.' You know what bunk is?" [Williams asked.]

"A lot of foolishness and trouble."

"You know you are here because you plead [sic] guilty?"

"Yes."

"You admit that you lied to the Chaplain—this gentleman over here?"

"Did I admit I lied to him?"

"Didn't you tell a lie to him inside?"

"I told him about—"

"The chaplain said you lied to him?"

"Yes."

"That is right?"

"Yes."

"He lied to me in this respect that he was there," [Chaplain Reed explained.]

"You lied to Father O'Brien?" [Williams asked.]

"No sir, I haven't lied to him."

"I have nothing else," [said the state attorney.]

[Neither had board member Edge. Bill Marsteller, however, asked to make a statement to the board. But before he could speak, Dan Williams said:]

"I was going to say, you are here and have you exhausted all the judicial proceedings in this case?"

"We had, up until this confession came out," [replied Marsteller.] "Last Wednesday the supreme court denied our motion for leave to file a petition in error."

"How [sic] do you mean by 'this confession?," [Williams asked.]

"I learned of this confession by Chaplain Reed, who wrote a letter on Saturday morning. On Thursday prior to Saturday morning we had filed with the Governor a request that this case be examined because Joe Weaver was being sent to the electric chair on the uncorroborated testimony of Alex and that his sentence be commuted to life."

"Without his testimony, he couldn't have been convicted?" [Edge asked.]

"Absolutely not," [Marsteller said.]

[Board member Williams asked the Plaintiff attorney whether he had already notified the prosecuting attorney about the confession.]

"Yes sir," [Marsteller replied.] "When we got Chaplain Reed's letter, Saturday morning, I immediately went to the Prosecuting Attorney and gave him that letter. Saturday morning we gave him the letter immediately upon receipt of it."

"You notified the Judge?"

"We called the Judge at Norwalk where he is sitting by assignment and also wrote a letter to him."

"What was his response?"

"His response was that if such were true he feels the man should be granted a new trial. And his advice to us was to file a motion for new trial on newly discovered and perjured testimony."

[Dan Williams asked Marsteller whether it was he or Cook who had the conversation with the judge. Nathan Cook responded. He and the judge had talked long distance on Saturday morning from his office. William Marsteller added:]

"We were asking at that time that the Governor commute the man to life rather than the chair. We do not ask that now. At this time we ask this board to give the courts an opportunity to investigate this, but in the meantime, that the Governor grant a stay from January 20th until such time as the court can take judicial notice of this case and review it, for if this man is telling the truth, we don't want Weaver sent to the electric chair on the sole testimony of this man.

"When I say sole testimony," [Marsteller said,] "I want to say this man was convicted—with the exception of two streetcar conductors, these two men, some passenger who got on the car about five miles from there and got off within three or four blocks of the plan [sic] and another streetcar conductor who said they got on the car at 10:30, which was before the time the man was killed—because Jasper Russel [sic] punched the A. D. T. Telegraph box at the plant at 10:30; that register absolutely to the minute.

"The conductor says this man got on his car at 10:30, not 10:31, or 10:29, I might say uncorroborated except these two men. They couldn't have made the case to go to the jury—the state couldn't— without this man's testimony, this man's testimony alone.

"We ask this opportunity and that the Governor will grant a stay from Friday until the court can take notice of this case."[161]

The next day, the state supreme court was presented with another motion from the defense, one that alleged error and challenged the methods the police had used in obtaining Alex Mayner's confession. The court denied the motion; however, on the strength of Alex's statement and the board's recommendation, Governor A. V. Donahey granted a 30-day reprieve until February 20th. Immediately, the Plaintiffs filed for a new trial, claiming newly discovered evidence. Judge Carpenter said he would announce his decision on their motion on February 6th. That would allow time, he said, for Alex's testimony to be investigated.

Told about the developments at the hearing, *Gazette* editor Harry Smith forged ahead, insistent in his trenchant little publication that...

> ...the city, the county, or the state should pay and pay big for the harrowing experience Joseph Weaver has had ever since his first arrest on the false charge of murdering Jasper Russell.
>
> Did the fact that Russell and the jury were white and Weaver and Maynor colored have anything to do with this awful miscarriage of justice? To say the least the verdict of the jury is open to much criticism, and Attorneys Cook and Marsteller are deserving of unstinted praise for saving Weaver's life, practically at their own expense.[162]

The state attorneys countered with a motion of their own. They charged on February 6th that Judge Carpenter did not have the authority to consider such a motion by the Plaintiffs because his term of office had expired. The judge was in no position to disagree, and struck the petition for a new trial from the files. Therefore, the jury decision at trial stood.

Cook and Marsteller wasted no time in taking the matter to a higher court, but their effort was thwarted by the appellate court's affirmation of Judge Carpenter's decision. The higher court said the trial judge had acted according to law, newly discovered evidence notwithstanding.[163]

CHAPTER 11

LETTERS FROM A COLUMBUS PRISON

Harry Clay Smith's little newspaper of 45 years enjoyed popularity among black Americans. It had readers from ocean to ocean and from the Great Lakes to the great Gulf. Except for the first two years of his life, Smith was a lifelong resident of Cleveland. He had been elected to three Republican terms in the Ohio general assembly. He could boast of sponsoring two significant laws that benefited the state's black population.

> His Anti-Mob Violence Law of 1894 was designed to check the lynching spirit which, by the 1890's, was assuming the proportions of a national menace. This act made the county responsible for public order, and its indirect effect was to stimulate law-enforcement officials in the prevention of mob action. Smith's Civil Rights Law of 1896 made discrimination in public places, based on race or color, illegal; and this law was enforceable by civil and criminal court action.[164]

Just age 20 when he founded a newspaper with three associates, Smith became sole owner and editor before long. Beginning with the first issue of August 25, 1883, he made sure his "Old Reliable" *Gazette* hit the street every week and hit on time. Proud of his publication with a $2.00 yearly subscription price, Editor Smith ran a perennial message to his readers: *Character, like a fine old tree, matures slowly and is a riper growth than success that is forced as hothouse products are forced. Character in a newspaper develops through years of service to the people....*

By 1892, Smith had organized the Afro-American Republican Club and had served as its first president. An orator of persuasive ability, he had placed fifth in 1926 among twelve candidates in the primaries for Republican gubernatorial nominee. He lost big that year but was comfortable in the role he perceived of himself— that of trail blazer for black gubernatorial candidates of the future.

After Alex Mayner changed his story, Prosecutor Stanton made a trip to the state house in Columbus.

> Tuesday, Prosecutor Edward C. Stanton of Cuyahoga County complained to the governor that the repudiation had aroused public sentiment in favor of Weaver and "created the idea that an innocent man has been accused unjustly" and he believed "the public would lose confidence in our institutions and in the machinery for the enforcement of law."[165]

Afterward, Stanton went over to West Spring Street and talked with the chaplain and the warden. Then he met with the convicted man, and finally, the accuser.

Stanton left still convinced of Weaver's guilt, but told reporters he would recommend the Governor change the sentence to life imprisonment. His concern was, he said, the public's faith in capital punishment. He feared it would be shaken by the condemned man's execution at that time. Governor Donahey ordered written reports from the warden and the chaplain, their own investigations into Mayner's confession.[166]

Assistant Prosecutor James Connell told the press that the Governor saw the facts as pointing to Weaver's guilt. The chief of the state regarded the lifer's confession as a "sentimental outburst." He agreed with Prosecutor Stanton that electrocuting the questionably accused man at that time would be a blow to capital punishment in Ohio. Connell said the Governor ought to commute the sentence to life. There was no doubt in the assistant prosecutor's mind that Weaver was guilty. But as long as there was doubt in the lay mind, he said, it would not be fair to let Weaver die.[167]

On February 17, 1928, three days before the Governor's reprieve expired, the supreme tribunal of the state granted Joe Weaver an indefinite stay.

Harry Smith placed the welfare of his people above his own personal and business affairs. His was a never-ending charge "against any national, state, or municipal legislation that was inimical and harmful discrimination in its effect upon his people. No cringing, no toadying, no sidestepping, and no Jim Crowing in his program...," in the assessment of an unnamed colleague who said further:

> "Smith is singular, rugged, forceful, dynamic, full of consuming fire that always flames hot to singe every defamer of his race and spurts unceasingly at every vestige of race discrimination. There is nowhere in these [sic] United States a more uncompromising champion of equal rights and privileges for his people than Harry C. Smith."[168]

It was to this unflinching champion that prisoner No. 57064 turned for help.

> Dear Mr. Smith: I received *The Gazette*, printed on Saturday, January 21, 1928. It contained the pictures of my attorneys, the Chaplain and me. I am delighted to have them and all others see that you are taking a stand for righteousness and justice.
>
> I suppose you know that the decision in my case hasn't been handed down by the supreme court as yet. I believe the court will grant me a new trial. It has been proven already from the confession of Alex Maynor that I and my witnesses told the court the truth when we swore that I had no part in the crime....He did not have a hard job of putting it on me because the policemen helped him.
>
> They framed me from A to Z. The policemen could have learned the truth in the beginning if they had looked into the matter as carefully as they should have done.

Many, many thanks for your kindness. It eases my mind to read your paper's eloquent plea for justice for me and I am greatly encouraged by its firm stand for justice and liberty for an innocent man. Also to know that we still have some real men in our race. Many men of both races had laid down their lives for the right, justice and liberty. I am

Yours truly, Joseph Weaver[169]

In the section for the condemned, a death row guard was tuned in to irksome news. The Cleveland Indians had been defeated by the New York Yankees in exhibition baseball. The score tied at *one* going into the ninth inning, Babe Ruth had stepped up to the plate with the bases loaded. He blasted one out of the park in Sarasota, Florida, much to the chagrin of an Indians fan sitting in his cell within earshot of the radio. The hard news of the day followed the sports report.

"In Columbus today, the supreme court acted again on the case of Joe Weaver, convicted Cleveland killer who is awaiting death in the electric chair. Previously, the court had refused Weaver a new trial. But his attorneys, Nathan E. Cook and William F. Marsteller, re-opened the case because of the recent confession of Alex Mayner, whose testimony was largely responsible for Weaver's conviction. Mayner, now serving life, confessed recently that he had framed Weaver. In reality, Mayner said, Weaver had absolutely nothing to do with the murder...."[170]

The supreme tribunal of the state had granted an indefinite stay on February 17th. This action gave the court time to deliberate on the motion vigorously argued by Joe Weaver's attorneys.

If an ember of support for northern justice flickered below the Mason-Dixon line, Nate Cook was bent on inflaming it. He got off a letter to the white owner-editor of the weekly newspaper that circulated in Joe's home county. Roy McElmurray published Cook's plea in the *True Citizen*, and prefaced the letter with an appeal of his own.

The case of the State of Ohio vs. Joseph Weaver was heard Thursday at Columbus, Ohio, and Messrs. Cook and Marsteller were present to present evidence to stay the execution of Joseph, whose date of execution is set for Monday, the 20th. These young men have stood by the negro [sic] boy in his fight all the way through and are strongly convinced of his innocence. We took the liberty of publishing Mr. Cook's letter…to show our people that an unfair fight, it seems, is being made against the negro on account of prejudice. These gentlemen have been faithful and are making every effort in behalf of Weaver.

The Citizen suggests that, whatever the outcome of the case, the negroes take up a collection among Weaver's friends to assist the men who have had to carry the burden of expenses involved in fighting for his life. A number of our white citizens will help with the contribution, and raise an amount worthy to be sent, and *The Citizen* in accordance with this suggestion starts the list with $5. Let others follow suit.

The True Citizen ——————————$5.00.

Cleveland, Ohio, February 10th— Mr. W. L. McElmurray, Waynesboro, Ga.

Dear Mr. McElmurray:

Your valued favor of February 8th, with reference to the case of the State of Ohio vs. Joseph Weaver, has been received.

Mr. William F. Marsteller and I were appointed by the State of Ohio to defend Weaver last April, because Weaver stated to the Court that he had no funds with which to employ counsel. Weaver's trial lasted one week; the jury found him guilty upon practically uncorroborated testimony of Alex Maynor, another colored boy, and Weaver was sentenced to the electric chair. The State of Ohio paid us for our work up to this point. Immediately after Weaver was sentenced, Maynor confessed his guilt and was rewarded for having testified against Weaverr [sic] by being given life imprisonment. Neither Mr. Marsteller nor myself were convinced of Weaver's guilt in spite of the jury's verdict and as time has gone on we have become more firmly convinced each day of Weaver's absolute innocence.

We had a transcript of the testimony made, which cost us $340.00. We carried his case through the Court of Appeals of this county and the Supreme Court of the State of Ohio, which sits at Columbus, Ohio, one hundred fifty miles from here. We have been to Columbus a half dozen times. Both the Court of Appeals and the Supreme Court sustained the conviction. Joe Weaver was sentenced to be electrocuted on August 12th, 1927, and while we were going through the Court of Appeals and the Supreme Court it was necessary for us to obtain many stays of execution until the Courts could decide the matter. We have prepared numerous briefs, done a great deal of investigation and been put to a great deal of expense, such as hotel bills, travelling, telegrams, etc. On January 6th the case was argued before the Supreme Court and the conviction was sustained by them and they fixed the date of execution as of January 20th. We then filed a petition with the Governor asking that Joe Weaver's penalty be commuted from the electric chair to life imprisonment.

Shortly after the hearing of the Supreme Court and after our petition to the Governor, this other negro [sic] man, Alex Maynor, told the Chaplain of the penitentiary that Weaver was not with him and that Weaver took no part in the murder and was an innocent man; that he had testified that Weaver committed the murder in order to save himself from the electric chair. Immediately after this confession on the part of Maynor, the Chaplain notified us. We immediately went to Columbus to investigate this and were able to get it before the Board of Clemency. We attended that hearing and the Board of Clemency recommended to the Governor that a stay of execution for thirty days be granted to permit an investigation of Maynors' [sic] confession. We then returned to the County Court and filed a motion for a new trial on the grounds of newly discovered evidence, but two terms of Court having passed since Weaver was convicted, the prosecutor has filed a motion to dismiss our motion for a new trial and the judge informs us that in his opinion he has no jurisdiction in the matter, and, under the law of Ohio, we feel that the judge is right.

However, if the judge refuses our motion for a new trial, we shall carry this to the Suprerme [sic] Court and test it out. We have filed an application for a rehearing of the case in the Supreme Court, which has been granted and which will necessitate our going to Columbus on February 16th and argue the case again. At the present time it looks as though we will have to make from three to five more trips to Columbus before the case is thoroughly thrashed out in the Courts, and, if we lose in the Courts, we will then attempt to get him pardoned by the Governor and if unable to do that we will attempt to get the Governor to commute his sentence from the electric chair to life imprisonmen [sic].

The reason that we have fought Joe Weaver's case from the day the jury brought in a verdict of guilty of first-degree murder, is because we felt that this poor negro [sic] boy, without funds or friends, was an innocent man. We were so strong in our belief of his innocence that to date it has cost us one thousand dollars, not to take into consideration the time that we have spent in the case or any fee. You can therefore see that the burden has been quite heavy upon us and there is no provision in the laws of Ohio to reimburse us for the money we have spent or to remunerate us for the services we have rendered.

In answer to your question what you could do financially for Joe Weaver, we would like to say that if you and some of the citizens of your community would like to help us in carrying this heavy burden, we would greatly appreciate same.

Mr. Marsteller is a Kentuckian by birth and rearage and thoroughly knows the negro; he is convinced that Joe Weaver is innocent and that Alex Maynor is an awful liar, and he says that the prejudice against the negro in the northern part of Ohio is different than in the south [sic]; that Joe Weaver would have never been convicted in the south and that the biggest fight we have, [sic] is the northern prejudice against the negro [sic].

With very kindest regards and appreciation of your letter, I remain, Sincerely yours,

Nathan E. Cook[171]

Harry Smith's modest weekly publication was Joe Weaver's steady link to the world beyond the walls of his death cell. The condemned man learned through the "Old Reliable" that an increasing number of news dailies were taking up his cause, demanding on their editorial pages that fairness tip the scale of justice. They were calling upon fair-minded people of both races to act. Individuals as well as organizations across the state enlisted in the pursuit of justice. The Cleveland Association for Criminal Justice, for one, contacted the Governor with an offer to assist in a probe into the case should the courts fail to grant Weaver a new trial.[172]

Joe's night school teacher was among the enthusiastic supporters, as her note to the editor of the *Gazette* suggests: "I am especially happy over your interest in Joseph Weaver. He was my pupil in night-school and a very fine fellow. I was always particularly glad when he found it possible to attend. One more reason against capital punishment."[173]

Editor Harry Smith received another letter from death row.

My Dear Sir: I cannot refrain from writing you my thanks, appreciation and best regards after receiving and reading a copy of *The Gazette*, printed on Mar. 17th. It contained a copy of a letter that I wrote you explaining my condition and welfare. It would not take me over ten minutes to convince you of my innocence just as in the case of my attorneys, the penitentiary chaplain and about a half dozen deputies of the Cuyahoga jail, and dozens of others I talked with.

My foundation is God. He moved just in time. If it had not been for the prayers that were so constantly offered by me, my mother, relatives and different churches at my birthplace, down south [*sic*], and in Cleveland, especially the S. D. A. Church, Elder Dawson, pastor, I would not be alive today. Their volunteer mission-workers appointed a minister (Reverend A. N. Durant) of Columbus to visit me with prayers and to read passages of the scripture. Those ladies have my prayerful gratitude because it is the will of God that I should not die (an innocent man) in the electric chair. My case is still pending in the state supreme court.

Rest assured, Mr. Smith, that I am always glad to have a copy of *The Gazette* whenever it is convenient for you to send me one.

With best wishes I remain,
Yours very truly,

Joseph Weaver[174]

On April 12th, the state filed a motion of its own, theirs to strike down the Plaintiffs' February motion. Nine days later, Cook and Marsteller took the case back to the court of appeals.

The spring of 1928 blossomed with Joe Weaver still hopeful in his cell on death row. He wrote again to the *Gazette* editor.

Dear Sir: You have been so kind to me and sympathetic as to write to the Governor and publish many editorials and articles asking justice for me because you are of the opinion that I am innocent of the brutal crime that was "put over" on me. I take the greatest pleasure, this morning, in making a report to you again, because it is worth a fortune to me to read *The Gazette* which gives me much cheer.

My attorneys wrote me, recently, that they are still working hard for justice for me. Some white ladies of Cleveland, who are members of the W. C. T. U., and State legislators, say they will not leave anything undone in trying to see that I get justice. I know I will be a free man again because I am charged with another man's crime. My attorneys say they are expecting success in their latest effort to get me a new trial. The white ladies say that I may feel sure that I have many friends in Cleveland and that they are working hard for me.

Mr. Smith, if you have anything to say in regard to me in your later issues of *The Gazette*, I wish you would publish my sincere thanks and appreciation to the missionary volunteer society of The Seventh Day Adventist church, E. 71st St., and Cedar Ave., for ten dollars raised in a collection and given my attorneys. The S. D. A. church raised that amount for me after reading about me in *The Gazette*. My church in Georgia, and some others down there are doing the same thing. Oh, how much help it would be to me if all the other churches of Cleveland would give as much as the missionary workers of the Seventh Day Adventist church did to help a poor innocent man obtain a fair and square deal. My attorneys say I could demand speedier justice but for the lack of funds.

I have nothing to fear because the Lord has kept a guardian-angel watching over me, by day and by night, as he watched over Daniel in the lion's den. My endless thanks, Mr. Smith, for the acts of Christian kindness you have rendered me.

Yours in Christ,

Jos. Weaver[175]

The glare of summer lessened, the shadows of fall lengthened as the 1928 election appeared on the horizon. Harry Smith had finished in the middle of the pack of candidates for Republican nomination in 1926. Still, the unbowed trailblazer made another sprint for high political office. Support for his run for the gubernatorial position came from death row.

My Dear Mr. Smith: Thank you very much for the copies of "The Good Old Reliable *Gazette*" you have so frequently sent to me, free of charge, for the last eight months.

They give me the greatest of pleasure to read. In a group of pictures in the Columbus papers, I saw your picture and name, a candidate for the Republican nomination for Governor of Ohio. I admire you and am glad to see the commendable stand you take for the uplift of our race as well as the white.

I wrote you a letter, weeks ago, congratulating you on your firmness, which I hope you received. I was an active voter, myself, when at liberty. I am sorry I was unable to support you in the recent primary, but wished you success.

I regard you as my truest friend. It shows that you are standing up for justice, and that you are convinced of my innocence of a crime that was put over on me by false accusers. I will never forget the kindness you did me by writing the Governor in my behalf.

I am thankful to God that He knows as well as I know I am innocent of the crime. If I die in the electric chair or if I am never free again, my conscience is perfectly clear and I am thankful to God that not one drop of that man's blood is on my hands. I am yet in the best of hope and greatest confidence that I will be granted a new trial, and that it will be proved without a doubt that I am absolutely innocent of the crime that I was sentenced to die for.

In God we trust. I beg to remain,
Yours sincerely,

Joseph Weaver[176]

Dan Gallagher, staff correspondent of the *Cleveland News*, paid a mid-October visit to the chaplain's office in the penitentiary. Thomas O. Reed banged his fist on his desk and declared:

"Joseph Weaver will never go to the electric chair—you may depend upon that.

"If it has to be done, I, myself, will head a movement to prevent it, for I am thoroughly convinced that Weaver had no hand in the killing of Jasper Russell....

"Weaver is over there in the death cell and the gallant fight those Cleveland attorneys have made to save his life is deserving of the commendation of the people of this state. They have worked long and hard. And they have done it without pay.

"Why? Because they know it would be a crime to permit this man to go to the chair. I'm proud of the fact that Ohio has such attorneys.

"I have got myself in trouble because of my championship of the cause of this condemned man. But though additional trouble may come, I will not sit silent and let an innocent man go to his death....

"My interest in this case was aroused months ago when Judge Carpenter, who seemed to have had his doubts about the verdict being justified, appeared at this prison and made some inquiries. Following that, I was the guest of Warden Preston E. Thomas at dinner. And I told the warden: 'I want to get your permission to bring Maynor and Weaver together.' The warden gave me that permission. While I was taking Maynor to Weaver's cell in the condemned section I said to him: 'If Weaver is innocent, for God's sake say so.' That is all I said to him.

"What followed: Why, Maynor declared that he had lied at the trial; that Weaver had no hand in that murder. He expressed remorse for having sworn falsely on the witness stand. He named another man as the slayer. Later he repudiated that confession. Nevertheless, I know that Weaver is innocent. And because of his innocence I have told Warden Thomas 'If the time ever comes that Weaver starts a march to the electric chair, you will have to get some other chaplain to accompany him. For I will not be a party to such a miscarriage of justice.'

"I tell you I am going to launch a tremendous fight to save Weaver. As I understand it, his case is before the supreme court. If it is ordered that the death penalty be carried out, I will take his case to the people of Ohio. I'll head the movement to have justice accorded him. Mark my words: Joseph Weaver will never go to the electric chair.

"Claims have been made that I used 'unfair tactics' in connection with this matter. I deny that this is so. My sole aim has been to bring out the truth. And the truth has been forthcoming.

"I have witnessed 90 electrocutions. I have led 70 men from the cells to the electric chair. And never before have I positively felt that an innocent man was in danger of death, that the state was about to commit a disgraceful crime. At the time that I first protested Weaver's innocence I did not know that doubt existed in the mind of the judge who sentenced him. I have since found this to be true. Alex Maynor...confessed that he accused Weaver in order to escape the chair himself."[177]

Sunday evening, October 29, 1928, six convicts lay drowsily on cots in their cells in the death row cell block, their stomachs stretched from a sumptuous feast. In the quiet passageway beyond their cells, a guard paced in and out of shadows cast by feeble autumnal sun rays.

John Sabo had turned 21 that day. Three years older than when he was convicted of murder. In his defense he had maintained that he was at home the night of the slaying.

At 15, John had left Budapest for the States to join his mother, who had made it through before the door closed to European immigration because of the War. Together, mother and son had moved to Ohio. They were Akronites but three years when John's life changed forever.

Shortly after midnight on May 26, 1926, a 31-year-old rubber worker rang out at the B.F. Goodrich plant. His time card registered 12:08. At the corner of Huron and West Bartges Streets, not far from home, he paused under a broken street light to cut a plug of chewing tobacco.

Before he could put the knife back into his pocket, his assailant stepped from the shadows where he had been lurking and pulled the trigger of a small automatic pistol placed close to the plant worker's chest. The bullet punctured Barton C. Painter's right lung and lodged in his left shoulder. At 12:45, a city bus rolled up to the intersection to shine on the body that lay almost within sight of Painter's home where his wife and four-year-old daughter were asleep. The driver called police.

> [Some of the people questioned] believed the murderer killed the wrong man in the darkness. Others held the opinion Painter was killed by a highwayman who fired when he saw the pocket knife in Painter's hand.
>
> "Painter came here fourteen months ago from Whitleyville, Tennessee," [Detective Ed] McDonnell said. "He was known to his friends as a home lover and devoted to his wife and baby. So far as we could learn, he never had been in trouble with anyone and had not an enemy in the world. He seldom carried more than a dollar in his pockets.
>
> "This promises to be one of the most difficult crimes to solve we ever had been confronted with. Every possible clew is being investigated."

Painter's body will be returned to his former home in Tennessee for burial.[178]

Now 21, the young man convicted of killing Barton Painter celebrated his birthday by hosting a party for five of his condemned fellows. Folding chairs were brought in for them, a guard, and a trusty friend to use. The feast table was set up in the corridor outside their cells.

Several stays of execution already on file, inmate number 56989 sat at the head of the table enjoying the banquet arranged for him by "Mother" Thomas. Around his neck was the gift the warden's wife had given him—a perky tie as bright as his twinkling blue eyes. Graciously, he heaped up generous portions of spring chicken, dressing, and sweet potatoes for his uncommon guests. (Inmates in Columbus ate well.)

At John's right sat Stanley Hoppe, sullen, gazing into his plate, muttering something about newspaper men being present. Hoppe's execution was coming up the next Friday. He had been convicted of murdering a seven-year-old Toledo girl.

At one end of the table sat Everett Koon, grinning with but one week of life left. A jury had found him guilty of beating a Marion man to death during an attempted burglary. He had used a rock in the killing.

To John's left sat Joe Weaver, John Bradshaw, and John Rucker. Bradshaw was on his way to the chair for the murder of a Columbus man; Rucker for the murder of a Cincinnati patrolman during an attempted holdup.

In the center of the table, topping off the gastronomical treat, was a cake with 21 yellow candles sunk into white icing. Plenty of piping hot coffee was on hand to gingerly slurp. After-dinner cigars mellowed out the occasion.

Father O'Brien, a Catholic priest rarely seen without a cigar, had visited the celebrators before the party to lead them in prayer and grace before they ate.

And heartily they had eaten.[179]

Unsuccessful in his bid for statewide office, Harry Smith stayed the course as producer of the "Old Reliable" *Gazette*. In mid-November, Joe Weaver wrote to him again.

Dear Sir: This is to let you know that I received the copy of *The Gazette* on the 10th of this month, as you have been donating me weekly for the last ten months, and I cannot explain how glad I was to read how firm you are yet standing for justice for me though your fight is not new because you even wrote the Governor, last winter, asking for my freedom because you are convinced of my innocence. If there had been about a score [of] other prominent persons of Cleveland stood up as strong for an innocent man as you have, with the meager evidence that is pretended to be held against me, in all probability I would have been free eight months ago. I feel disappointed for not having received the assistance of the N. A. A. C. P. [sic] branch of Cleveland before which I put my complaints, more than six months ago, but they have turned me a deaf ear.

But I am glad to say that Attys. N. E. Cook and Wm. F. Marsteller, of 518 Leader Bldg., along with you have not left me comfortless. Mr. Cook and Mr. Marsteller have spent not less than $1000 in my defense just because they saw that a rotten and an unfair deal was given me.

On Nov. 13th, I had the [sic] visit from Reverend and Mrs. E. A. Clarke, the former a former [sic] pastor of St. John's A. M. E. Church, Cleveland. He is now pastor of St. Paul's A. M. E. Church, Columbus. Mrs. Clark [sic] was my former teacher at night at the Rutherford B. Hayes school, E. 40th and Central Ave.

I learned that my case will be up in the court of appeals in Cleveland on Nov. 26th. I am expecting to be free immediately after then. If the courts deny me a new trial, I believe that our associations will step to the front for justice for an innocent member of the race, and the chaplain of this institution declares he will lead.

The headline, "O. P. Chaplain Strong for Weaver" that you had in your paper of Nov. 10th, means a fortune for my liberty, and beside from that you are asking all who will to write the Governor for my release as you have already done.

Many, many thanks to you. I cannot thank you as my heart desires. I am,

Yours very truly,

Joseph Weaver[180]

CHAPTER 12

CRY, "JUSTICE!"

The editor and the judge stood in agreement on one key point: That the verdict in the Jasper Russell murder case had been reached by a jury that had taken one man's word over the other.

Joining the fray, the *Cleveland News* on its editorial page challenged the state to:

> ...either electrocute or free the obscure colored man languishing on death row, a black man who lacks both money and influence.... A compromise decision, sentencing the man to life imprisonment, is out of the question.
>
> Either Weaver must go free or he must be executed. Endless delay, however, is inexcusable. Four times Weaver has escaped the chair by a hair's breadth. He still remains in the shadow of death, in spite of the repeated expressions of doubt by the judge who presided at the trial, his attorneys, the Chaplain who is required to accompany him to the electric chair, and the declaration of Alex Maynor, the principal in the crime.
>
> The real test of justice is that it must be no respecter of persons. The Weaver case furnishes Ohio with a perfect set of circumstances to try the law's impartiality. If an error has been made, let it be rectified. There has already been time for a dozen thorough investigations by competent authorities.
>
> Weaver should be released or he should be executed—and without further delay.[181]

The handling of justice in Cuyahoga County fueled an ongoing controversy that straddled the Mason-Dixon line. Such dissonance in the Weaver case was used by a southern editor to further prop up his region's anti-migration arguments.

> The people of the East and Middle West are resenting more and more the migration of the Negro. No doubt Weaver will die or spend the rest of his life in prison—guilty or not, but the facts in this case should teach us something. The greatest of these is the home is the best place on earth and that the Negro now contemplating migration should ponder this. Then, too, he should remember the remarks made by the leader of the race a few years ago in our court house, when Dr. Morton [sic—Moton] of Tuskegee Institute advised the Negro of Burke County to stay on the farm, work hard, save his money, and buy him a farm of his own; then he would be a credit to his race and command respect in his community.

> To this Weaver replied succinctly in his diary: *If this had a-happened in Georgia on March 13, 1927, I would have been hangin' on some tree by March 16th*....[182]

There was faint doubt that Edward Stanton would be re-elected to a fifth term as county prosecutor in 1928. He had already held that office longer than any other person ever in the county. But Stanton chose to retire with what one of the afternoon papers called a:

> "Glorious" Record.
> County Prosecutor Stanton insists he will retire from office with a "glorious record of achievement...."
> Let us, then, examine the record.
> More than five years ago the Cleveland Association for Criminal Justice declared that "perhaps the most potent as well as the most prevalent enemy to criminal justice is perjury." Further, the association said, "the perjurer deserves the relentless pursuit of the protectors of the public."

What has Mr. Stanton done to "pursue" perjurers in this county? Practically nothing. The only real blow ever given perjury here came through the activities of a special prosecutor selected for the task because Stanton had fallen down on his duty.

For these five years perjury has continued to wax stronger and more arrogant. Lawyers and judges have commented on it; civic organizations have demanded its eradication. The initiative and referendum process, designed to safeguard popular government, has been virtually destroyed as an effective device in this county by perjury.

So much for perjury. Stanton of the "glorious record" was not interested....

Last year Cleveland established the highest murder rate in its history. Nine persons for each 100,000 were victims of unjustified homicide. Between March 1, 1925, and Sept. 30, 1926, four policemen were killed on duty.

There is, of course, a direct relationship between crime rate and the official vigor shown in the prosecution of criminals. During 1927 Mr. Stanton's office handled 1,439 felony cases. Of these 888 pleaded guilty; 551 denied their guilt. Of the 551, the grand jury, under the direction of the county prosecutor, indicted on 310, although every one of the 551 had come to the county from the Municipal Court.

Three hundred and ten, then, survived the preliminaries and were due for prosecution by Stanton. Of this number the prosecutor dismissed without trial 78; juries found 87 not guilty. This left 145 of the 551 to be tried who were successfully prosecuted and found guilty; a 26 percent achievement for Stanton of the "glorious record...."[183]

When he announced his retirement at 40, the formidable prosecutor said, "A man can stand up under all this and do it every day. But you go just so far and then you're done."

He would not run again "in '28 because the grind just got too hard."

The month after Stanton passed up certain re-election, Joe Weaver got off another letter to Harry Smith.

Dear Sir: With greatest of pleasure I received the letter, a few hours ago, which you sent me, that you received from the Governor, replying to one you wrote him asking for freedom for me because you are convinced of my innocence of a crime that I am yet under the sentence of death for. My heart leaped for joy to see that you are doing all you can to force the wheel to a speedy turn for justice for me.

If the person that committed the crime that was falsely charged to me had died in the electric chair to pay for it, I don't think his death would have been too severe punishment. And if I was guilty I should be willing to pay the debt. But since I am not guilty of the thot [sic] of degrading myself by an atrocious crime of the kind, I have no more right to die in the electric chair than I have to spend the balance of my life in the penitentiary. And since I believe the Governor will view my case in this direction, he will not want to hold me in prison if a few persons ask for my liberty as you have done....

Alex Maynor was a roomer of mine for five or six months in 1926 but he had quit rooming with me about six months prior to the man's death. In his confession exonerating me, he admitted he told me while living with me that he once was a regular freight-train hobo and was held by federal authorities of Cleveland for transporting moonshine in 1926 or 1925, and that he killed his wife at his original home, Nashville, Tenn., in the year of 1912.

Thank you again, Mr. Smith for your continued efforts to help get justice for me. With best wishes I am

Yours truly,

Joseph Weaver[184]

Chaplain Reed decided he had waited long enough. It was time to take the Weaver case as he knew it to the public. Convinced of the condemned man's innocence, he spoke before the Sam S. Voucher Club of Cleveland at Euclid Avenue Baptist Church, and declared his intention to urge the Federation of Women's Clubs of Ohio to campaign for commutation of the sentence to life imprisonment.

An editor at one of the afternoon papers (cited in Smith's weekly) sought a different judicial remedy.

> Chaplain Reed's plan to interest the Federation of Women's Clubs of Ohio in a campaign to obtain commutation of sentence for Weaver seems to us, however, to be an incorrect step.
>
> If Weaver is guilty, commutation is not warranted. If he is innocent, he should be freed. If there is grave doubt in the minds of those closely connected with the case and thoroughly conversant with all its details, Weaver should be granted a new trial. Life imprisonment is hardly a sensible compromise between the death penalty and complete freedom. But so long as the element of doubt troubles not only his legal representatives, giving of their time without hope of compensation, Weaver's execution would be a grave miscarriage of justice. If the death penalty is to continue as an effective deterrent against crimes of violence, it cannot be authorized when there lurks even the faintest suspicion that a condemned man is actually guiltless.
>
> In the Weaver case, there is obviously more than a suspicion....[185]

Another letter was delivered to the *Gazette* office. It was an appeal to the community.

> Dear Sir:
> Ever since I've been here, since I had no other job, I've been writing for other men as many of them cannot write for themselves.
> Among the number is John Sabo, a young Hungarian in poverty like myself. He is new in this country and knows very little of the English language. It is believed, even by some of the State officers, that Sabo is innocent of the crime he is under sentence of death for. And since the Hungarian people are of the same conviction, word to that effect has been circulated among Hungarian American citizens by Hungarian newspapers. John Sabo's evidence proving his innocence isn't half as strong as mine. And yet, let me tell you that money from nearly every state in the union has been raised

by the Hungarian people and sent to the treasurer of the fund for him at the headquarters in Akron to help him demand justice.

Total amount, over $4,000. Our newspapers have published repeatedly the fact that I am an innocent man and about to be executed. Our race seems to believe they have more and better religion than any other race on earth, and I feel ashamed while answering not less than 800 Sabo letters, since I have been helping him, thanking the Hungarian people for what they are doing to help him, not more than a few, out of the ten million of our people in this country, have made a move to help me and those few consist of the Mission Volunteer society of the Seventh Day Adventist church. ...Reverend Dr. Clarke and his family of Columbus..., you and a few others.

Attys Cook and Marsteller asked me after I was "convicted," did I have any money to pay for carrying my case up to the higher courts. I told them no. They said since we are convinced of your innocence, we are going to spend our own money and look to your people to pay us if they can.

Thanks, thanks to the highest, for the stand you and others have taken for me, an innocent man. I am

Yours sincerely,

Joseph Weaver[186]

Though editorially in agreement with his counterpart at the *News*, Harry Smith doubted that the attorneys could get a second trial. The *Gazette* editor pressed for another remedy.

...Weaver, an innocent man, must be given his freedom, either as a result of a new trial or through pardon by the Governor. His execution would be more than "a grave miscarriage of justice." This state cannot afford and we do not believe it will permit such a blot on its escutcheon. Our people, at least, should never cease writing Gov. A. V. Donahey, State House, Columbus, O., requesting him to pardon Joseph Weaver, until that innocent man is given the freedom and liberty he has been deprived of now for more than a year. It will be difficult to find a stronger or better argument against a continuance of the death penalty in this or any other State of the Union than this Joseph Weaver case. Write Governor A. V. Donahey to pardon Weaver. Do YOUR duty![187]

Anna V. Hughes of Columbus headed the Legislative Committee of the Ohio Federation of Our Women's Clubs. Hers was an open letter of appeal to all of her club chapters. Harry Smith gave the letter of December 17, 1928, a prominent headline—*Save Weaver! Our Women Call!*

Dear Club Members: Joseph Weaver is still in the death row of the Ohio Pen. Honorable Harry C. Smith, editor of *The Gazette*, is doing splendid work in keeping before the public the case of this young man.... The Welfare League of Cleveland, Mr. Charles White, president, Cleveland NAACP, and Walter F. White of the New York office in attendance at the Interdenominational Ministers Alliance at Cleveland stand ready to assist. Mrs. Dovie King Clarke, who formerly taught him [Joe Weaver] in the evening schools of Cleveland, is now visiting our various Ohio organizations in an effort to pass to these audiences her affection for her former pupil, feeling that to anyone who has known him closely, it is unthinkable to connect him with a sordid crime.

The greatest anxiety now prevails to get this matter properly before Gov. Donahey at once because only a few days remain of his administration. I am asking that our clubs show co-operation by writing him letters at once, asking for the pardon of Joseph Weaver. Do not wait for regular meetings of your clubs but get together on this at once. Gov. Donahey's term of office expires Jan. 14; the matter should be closed days before then. Let every club not only send a letter to the Governor, but influence ministers and influential persons and organizations to do the same—this month.[188]

Citizens from New York to Los Angeles responded to the newspaper editorial calls to action. Through letters and telegrams to the governor of Ohio they voiced concern for the carriage of justice in the Midwest. Mattie Spellman of Stand Products

Company on the East Coast believed the trial was unfair. She requested a pardon, as did six women in Los Angeles. Ohioans clamored for some form of clemency in petitions to the chief of the state. Some letters were finely written, others scrawled and barely intelligible. State officials were unabashedly coaxed. Folk of common education demanded freedom outright; the better educated cajoled with eloquence.

George Daniels, an attorney in Springfield said he was "convinced from the history of the case given in the press and testimonies of disinterested observers that Joseph Weaver is innocent." He requested an unconditional pardon, contending that the attorneys for the condemned man had overlooked a legal point which had proved detrimental in their efforts to secure a new trial.

H. S. Chauncey, President of the Empire Savings and Loan, asked further consideration for the case. He voiced the widespread feeling that a mistake was about to be made.

Organizations lent their names. The Ohio Federation of Colored Women, "five thousand strong," mailed in petitions to their legislators. The Alpha Phi Alpha fraternity's "three thousand college men" hinted at their voting strength.

One hundred members from the Laymen's League of Cuyahoga County signed a petition. Urging an immediate pardoning of Joe Weaver, it said:

> ...The 85,000 colored people in Cuyahoga County believe that you are a Governor chucked full of justice; that you always seek divine guidance in all momentous questions and therefore will grant this solemn request.[189]

The B. K. Bruce Voters League of Piqua sought to attune the governor to the prayers of thousands for executive clemency. Religious groups tactically routed heaven-bound petitions through the state capital. The Baptist Ministers Association, the Interdenominational Ministers' Alliance, and the Club of Colored Lawyers—all of Cleveland— announced the passage of strong resolutions to cooperate in any way to liberate Joseph Weaver.

The Culture Club Assembly Study of Springfield appealed to the governor to pardon the man based on his youth and the confession made by another of his innocence.

The De Vore Manufacturing Company of Columbus was one of the businesses that wrote to the chief of the state. Community organizations enlisted in the clemency effort: the Literary Club of Columbus, the Phyllis Wheatley Women's Federated Club of Wellsville, Ohio, and the Neighborhood Club of Wilberforce. The Club of Colored Lawyers made known their resolve to cooperate in any way to gain Joe Weaver's freedom. From the Negro Welfare Association of Cleveland (now on board after saying earlier in a letter that there was nothing they could do) to the New York office of the NAACP, civic organizations queued up, ready to help.

Race as a factor was addressed by many in solicitation. The state director of Motion Pictures of the Women's Christian Temperance Union suggested:

> Many jurors are, unconsciously perhaps, prejudiced against the negro [*sic*] accused of crime. I appeal to you to give immediate and careful attention in behalf of justice that the State of Ohio may not take the life of an innocent boy tho colored.[190]

Cook and Marsteller were in a dogfight with the prosecutors before the appellate court.

Under old established rules, a motion could not be filed for a new trial once the term of the court in which the conviction had taken place had expired.

In a gutsy move, Joe's advocates challenged the law itself. They latched on to an old test case that claimed a comma had been left out of the Ohio Code. Omitted, the comma put men in the electric chair. Inserted, the Plaintiffs argued, the meaning changed enough to allow the courts to make exception for cases where trials were sought based on newly discovered evidence.[191]

Another letter from the death house found its way to Editor Harry Smith. It was dated December 21, 1928.

Kind Sir: I am writing you for the purpose of letting you know how glad I was to read the few lines on your card saying "we are doing our best for you, and are hopeful, too." I know if our people in Cleveland and Ohio lift up their voices for justice for me, along with my attorneys, I will be given my freedom.

I cannot help thinking how the assistant prosecutor, James C. Connell, of Cleveland, came down here, on the order of Prosecutor Stanton, last February, and came very near convincing the Governor that I was guilty, after Alex Maynor had exonerated me; and no doubt, at the same time, knowing better. He recommended life imprisonment, and that, I believe, to keep the Governor from blaming them for being careless as they were about the life of a person and his innocence.

The policemen sure find lots of pleasure in given [sic] a person the "third degree." They could easily have found the truth about the crime in the beginning. I can't understand how they thought I could have worked two days in succession following the death of the man, if I had killed him, and not knowing where Maynor was. Why that job for me would have been like sitting on a red hot stove. The policemen arrested me at work, on the job.

There is lots I would be glad to explain in a new trial (if I was given one) which would wipe out all doubts as to my innocence. There are about a half-dozen persons, who falsely testified against me, who will be locked up for perjury, if I am granted a new trial. The people I am referring to will have nothing to hide under, if I face trial again.

I was so bewildered and outdone to see how the policemen stood up and let Alex Maynor slip his awful deed over on me, if they did not assist him, until I hardly knew right from wrong part of the time.

I am in the best of hopes for freedom, believing as you say that you all will do the best you can for me. This is my first time to be in prison and it's my first time to ever be arrested.

Merry Xmas,

Joseph Weaver[192]

A letter from Joe also went to his attorneys to wish them a "Merry, merry Christmas." It ended with a postscript of simple logic:

> PS. Is it true that a little punctuation which we call the comma will be the only incident that can be found to bar an innocent person from a new trial?
>
> I wonder why don't they rub that comma out. I think that article of law should be regulated![193]

In imagery at odds with the holiday theme, reporter Arthur Brisbane offered a thought-provoking challenge in a feature article entitled "Speech and Thought Make Our Lives."

> We human beings ceased to be animals and became men when we first used thought in place of brute strength.
>
> At some distant day in our development the animal that preceded us here made up its feeble mind that there was something better than strength, teeth and claws, and began to use its little brain.
>
> This animal, our ancestor, the so-called pithecanthropus or monkey-man, observed the saber-tooth tiger ripping open the stomach of a monster three times its size, watched the mammoth ploughing through swamps, crushing down trees, observed the great reptiles and all other proofs of brute force, and without realizing it, this ancestor said vaguely to himself:
>
> "I can't compete when it comes to teeth and claws, weight and bulk, I am a feeble thing in this jungle of power and battle. I must think the way out."
>
> And so our real human life began.
>
> Our ancestor, with a forehead one-quarter inch high, a jaw that stuck out as far as the jaw of a gorilla, with teeth bigger than those of any bulldog, and with long arms dropping below the knees, that could crush a man of today with ease, this old ancestor of ours decided that he would get out of the battle for supremacy of muscle and teeth and see what could be done with the brain and thinking.
>
> You can imagine how the thinking process started.

161

It was hardly real thought at first, just a kind of intelligent impulse. Our ancestor sat up in a tree rubbing his nose and looking at the saber-toothed tiger that couldn't climb.

He saw the shining teeth, six inches long perhaps, and he didn't like the look of them.

Later, when the tiger was gone, he climbed down and picked up a sharp flint, ten inches long, heavier, sharper and harder than the tiger's tooth.

He had discovered that a tooth made of stone held at the end of an arm four feet long could do as much damage as the tooth of a tiger.

So he fastened his sharp flint to the end of a piece of wood, sat in the tree, stabbed the tiger in the back as he passed, broke his backbone, ate his flesh, took the teeth to make implements and ornaments for himself—and so began the thinking human race.

Later, man used explosive dynamite shells in place of sharp flints, he dwelt in skyscrapers in place of holes in the rocks, and he used flying machines in place of canoes dug out of a log.

But all the time he was a thinking animal instead of an animal relying on strength, teeth, muscle, thick hide, claws.

And every step that he gained in his upward climb toward control of the earth and dominion over the animals was gained by the thought that was started when he made up his mind to use the sharp flint and conquer the long white tooth.

A thinking man is a descendant of all the thinkers of 300,000 years past.

He comes in an unbroken line from the old half-monkey, half-thinking creature that discovered the possibility of conquering animals stronger than himself.

Readers, whether you be old or young, realize it now that your salvation, your hope, your chances in life, are all in the thinking power hidden away in your head.

To what extent can you make thought, recently acquired by men, control the animal forces and passions that date back millions of years to our earliest ancestors to solve your problems and protect yourself, and be a benefit to the human race, or are you to wait and waste, and wonder and delay, until it is too late, as with this man?[194]

Joe spent part of Christmas Eve of 1928 writing another letter to Harry Smith.

> Dear Sir: Pardon me for writing so often. But I cannot refrain from doing so after being so enthused since I read *The Gazette* of Dec. 22nd, and saw that you are reinforced by various organizations in your effort to help secure justice, which means freedom for me, as I am an innocent man. I was expecting them to move for me which I believe ought to be their duty.
>
> I noticed in *The Gazette* that you are urging every competent citizen who will to write the Governor at once asking him to pardon me. Well, it would be safer for me to be pardoned by the Governor than it will to take a chance on getting a new trial. However, one day seems as long as a week in here at times to me; but I'd rather spend two weeks overtime in here and be acquitted by a jury than to be pardoned by the Governor. That is because, if I am given another chance to make a statement to a jury, there will not be one doubt left as to my innocence.
>
> I cannot take vengeance upon anyone because that belongs to God. But there were a little more than a half dozen false witnesses against me at my trial who ought to be punished by a just law. Mrs. Holliday…Alex Maynor's wife's pal from her youth, sat in the witness chair with her eyes cast down upon her toes and swore to a willful [expletive deleted] by denying the truth…. It is true I was at Alex Maynor's house from ten to fourteen hours prior to the death of the man, and I could not deny that to the court. Mrs. Holliday was there, and since Maynor has betrayed her trust, he is my best witness against her in a new trial, if I get one. The streetcar conductors admitted to the court that they did not get interested about identifying anybody until they saw there was a thousand dollar reward offered for the killer of the man.
>
> There was lots left out in my trial that I wish to explain. I do not wish to publish it now, but that is why the policemen forced the charge against me. I will, sometime maybe, in the near future

explain it to you in a letter. I explained it to my attorneys, since I've been here.

Every word from start to finish at my "trial" was just a frame-up against me. Most anybody would have taken advantage of the opportunity to save his own life, as Maynor did, by going thru the gap that the policemen and others opened up for him in order to use him as their principal witness to convict me. I gave Alex Maynor my number and name on a piece of paper for the purpose of selling him some cloth to make his wife a suit to match one I had already sold him for $42.50. The policemen found that scrap of paper in his pocket when they arrested him and they used it for a clew to link me with Alex in the murder of that poor man. They came very near beating me to death; they were too unmerciful and brutal giving the "third degree" to tell. Alex Maynor said, while exonerating me, that the policemen beat him and made him say I was with him after they found my name on a piece of paper in his pocket. He said they knocked out one of his teeth and broke two of his ribs.

Yours sincerely,

Joseph Weaver[195]

While Joe Weaver wrote his Christmas letters, the appellate court was again looking at the Weaver case, the comma contention of no moment. The sole issue, as the court saw it, was whether or not the common pleas court could grant a new trial on a motion filed after the term of that court had expired, the term in which the judgment had been entered.

The appellate court stood firm on the negative. It held that the trial court had no jurisdiction to entertain the new trial motion. It affirmed the trial court's decision not to grant relief based on the discovery of the perjured testimony.

Instead of a pardon, in January, outgoing Governor Donahey granted Joe Weaver a reprieve until February 20th.

The state supreme tribunal looked at the Weaver case and the Sabo case in tandem. Both sets of lawyers were arguing the same question before the court. The Akron Plaintiff had affidavits to show that another man had confessed to killing Barton Painter, but the time for presenting the affidavits had passed. Thousands of John Sabo's countrymen and friends believed him innocent and were working tirelessly to save his life. In both men's cases, the attorneys claimed discovery of new evidence and hoped to convince the supreme court that it had an inherent duty to correct the mistakes lower courts made. But the prosecutors from both Cuyahoga and Summit counties stood fast in opposition. Limitless time for filing a motion for a new trial, they argued, opened the door to endless litigation.

In both cases, the court affirmed the judgments of the courts of appeal and pointed to the prohibitive statute of the law.[196]

That week, Editor Smith made a passionate plea to supportive *Gazette* readers.

> January 18, 1929 was the day we intended to carry the plea of our people of Ohio, and thousands of whites, to Columbus and ask the pardon of innocent Joseph Weaver had this not been made inadvisable and practically impossible by his case's being appealed to the state supreme court. Governor A. V. Donahey, whose last term expired January 14, 29, would have pardoned Weaver, too, had such action not been made impossible because of the pending action in Ohio's highest tribunal of justice. Tho a Democrat, Donahey was fair to our people throughout his six years as the chief executive of this state. He appreciated what they had done for him his last, triumphant election two years ago in November.
>
> As the matter now stands, the state supreme court having heard that last Friday the very earnest and strong plea of Weaver's untiring and manly attorneys, Messrs. Nathan Cook and William Marsteller, for a new trial, our people will be forced to appeal to the new Governor for a pardon for Joseph Weaver if the new trial is refused. The new evidence presented to the State Supreme Court, last week Friday, mainly the confession of the acknowledged murderer who is serving a life sentence in the Ohio Penitentiary for the commission of the crime, ought to secure the innocent man a new trial and God knows we and many thousands of others,

colored and white, here in Cleveland elsewhere in Ohio, hope and pray that it does.

Ohio cannot afford to electrocute and further imprison an innocent person or one whose alleged guilt is as greatly open to question and debate. Alex Maynor, the confessedly guilty person, now serving a life sentence in the Ohio Penitentiary, swears Weaver is innocent of the crime and that the latter was not even with him when the night watchman (white) was killed a year ago last fall [*sic*]. This alone ought to fully justify the granting of a new trial or a pardon either. But will it?

We sincerely and prayerfully hope so.[197]

The dogged attorneys filed an application for a rehearing before the state's highest court January 22, 1929. This time their application was unopposed by the prosecutor's office.

Meanwhile, in a Columbus death cell an invigorated man put pencil to paper with the editor of the *Gazette* in mind.

Dear Sir: I think it's about time to let you hear from me again. I am well and in the best of hope of being free again by spring, thru the help of our true and just God. As the result of constant prayers, He has guarded me for 21 months here in the death cell where so many guilty ones have fallen away into eternity from my side. But God has provided life for me until now because He knows I am innocent of the crime charged. If I was guilty Alex Maynor's statement exonerating me would not help me any because the testimony of his corroborating witnesses would uphold him. But no, all of them swore falsely against me and all of you can see how defective their statements are. I am in strong hopes of getting a new trial but I am still asking all your prayers.

I am greatly grieved to learn of the fall of Councilman Fleming. The sentence is from one to ten years here in the Ohio penitentiary. It's a good thing the jury that decided my case did not decide his.

Thanks to all, for the fight for me you are still waging, cooperating with my attorneys.

I receive *The Gazette*, every Saturday morning, which you have so kindly sent me for the last eleven months. Thanks for same. I am

Yours very truly,

Joseph Weaver[198]

Dovie King Clarke had moved to Columbus with the re-assignment of her husband, a Methodist preacher. The relocation made it easy for her to attend the rehearing. In a January 26th letter to the *Gazette*, the woman who had been Joe's night-school teacher reported on the positive atmosphere at the evidentiary hearing.

My Dear Mr. Smith: It occurs to me that I've been so busy trying to carry out your suggestions that I have failed to report as to the copies of *The Gazette* received by Miss Hughes and me, for free distribution. The Dec. 22 and 29 issues I rushed out over the state. I have given a few of the later issues out locally but thought to hold them back until our next campaign for sentiment.

I succeeded in getting some of our representative people to attend the Supreme Court hearing Jan. 18; Rev. Isom, Rev. Clarke, Mr. Gibson of The Supreme Life Ins. Co., now president of the local N. A. A. C. P. [*sic*]; Mr. and Mrs. Chas. Dickenson, officers of The N. A. A. C. P.; Mrs. Rosa Morman, founder of our Franklin Co. Women's Republican club; Mrs. Mayme Artis, member of the legislative department of our State Federation of clubs. The Weaver case was the last called. Atty. Marsteller at the stand. For the first time, that morning, the bench of judges unbent and gave a glint of personal feeling. Following a dialogue between Justice Jones and Attorney Marsteller, the Chief Justice said: "Mr. Marsteller, I think you see that you have one vote here, possibly others."

Judge Florence Allen was fine, too, in emphasizing certain favorable features (to Weaver) of the case. Attorney Marsteller was magnificent in his presentation of the case. And when the Chief Justice made the remark just quoted—no, it was in answer to Judge Jones, Marsteller replied: "Your Honor, you make me very happy saying so. This case is a pet of ours. Mr. Cook and I are using our time and money without a penny of pay because we believe in the innocence of our client."

When it was over, we all had something to say to the attorneys. They said that all that is needed is a new trial to establish beyond a doubt the innocence of their client. We came away hoping for the best for Joseph Weaver, and feeling that a movement should be started to reimburse the attorneys. I'm sure you will be one to do that in time. In the meanwhile, I have heard no news from the hearing; not anything further at all.

Yours sincerely,

(Mrs.) Dovie King Clarke[199]

Nothing further happened with the Weaver case until February 20, 1929, when the state supreme court took up the case. A key issue in the hearing was the .32-caliber bullet that killed Jasper Russell. Representing Joe Weaver, Marsteller contended that:

The evidence disclosed that Jasper Russell was killed with a 32-caliber bullet; that the revolver above mentioned was of that caliber. No revolver was found at the scene of the crime, nor in the possession or at the rooming place of either Weaver or Maynor, nor was the revolver, testified of by Weaver as being in the possession of Maynor, and denied by Maynor, ever found.

The question, therefore, whether Joseph Weaver had in his possession that night a revolver of that caliber or of any kind had an important bearing upon the probable guilt or innocence of Weaver.... The evidence was such that, giving equal credence to Weaver and Maynor, it was difficult to determine wherein even the preponderance lay. For Weaver was fairly corroborated as to his whereabouts during all that day and night by disinterested witnesses, apparently of the station and degree of intelligence and reliability of both Weaver and Maynor; the greater number of witnesses, the Plaintiff in error, and Maynor being Georgia negroes [sic].

The corroborating evidence of the two streetcar conductors, while tending to corroborate Maynor with reference to the trip out to the vicinity of the crime and back, was, by reason of certain facts developed at the trial, subject to the suspicion that it emanated from suggestion rather than recollection, however honestly believed by the witnesses themselves. So that the conclusion of guilt beyond a reasonable doubt could only have been arrived at by the process of wholly disbelieving the testimony of Weaver and believing the testimony of Maynor....[200]

The court then took up another matter raised by the Plaintiff against the state:

On the 16th, Wednesday, following the murder on Sunday, the police, unaccompanied by Weaver, went to his rooming house and took into custody his landlady, Evelyn Bedell, and her niece who was five years old the preceding September. At the trial Evelyn Bedell was subpoenaed by Weaver to testify as to his presence in her house during the evening and night of the 13th, which she did, and did not testify in chief as to any other matter.

Upon cross-examination she was asked [questions by the state about her niece; that is, what the police said to her and what she said to them].[201]

That was a procedural error, the court declared. The prosecution was not entitled to introduce a subject through Evelyn Bedell. She was not the state's witness, and the subject matter under question had not been introduced by the defense. Her testimony as evidence was hearsay and therefore incompetent. The court went on to state:

...There is no way of disguising the fact that the purpose of that part of the cross-examination of the witness Bedell, and of the direct examination of the witness Jacobs, was to bring to the attention of the jury the declarations of this five year old negro child, made in the absence of Weaver, made three days after the crime was committed, miles away from the scene of the crime.

And the fact that it was developed upon cross-examination under the guise of laying a foundation for impeachment, and was afterwards offered as impeachment, in no way justifies it....

With the testimony of Weaver and Maynor in conflict at every point, with each vitally interested in saving his own life, with some evidence corroborative of each, but not complete or conclusive as to either, the admission of the hearsay evidence in the record of the declarations of this five-year-old child, the only evidence in the record upon that subject, placing the gun that probably killed Jasper Russell in the possession of Weaver instead of Maynor, probably afforded that corroboration to the evidence of Maynor that enabled the jury to transform a grave doubt into a reasonable certainty and controlled its verdict.

That such evidence was not competent as substantive proof of the existence of a revolver at the time and place indicated by the hearsay evidence is so elementary that it need not be argued....[202]

The state's highest court reversed the judgment of the appeals court, set aside the verdict of the jury, and sent the cause back to the court of common pleas for a new trial. The decision was telegraphed to the prosecutor's office in Cuyahoga County. The realization of a new trial was quickly passed on to Harry Smith; his tabloid had a representative at that office.

In his weekly, the editor elaborated on the turn of events:

...This is certainly good news to many thousands of people of both races in Cleveland and throughout the state of Ohio, some of whom have been very active in Weaver's behalf for many weeks and months. A glorious victory that is sure to save the life of an innocent man who for many months has been incarcerated in the death cell of the Ohio penitentiary at Columbus. Our people of Ohio particularly, as well as Joseph Weaver, are very, very grateful for this relief and thank [the] Supreme Judges...and all the others who contributed in any way toward the granting of a new trial to Joseph Weaver.[203]

"This is one of the happiest days in my life," Nate Cook told reporters for Cleveland's dailies, who immediately pressed him and his partner with follow-up questions. "We are convinced that Weaver is innocent, and though there is not a cent of money in the case for us, we shall fight his battle for him until he gets justice and is finally free from this charge."[204]

Cook (who never lost a client to the electric chair) rang up Columbus and asked Chaplain Reed to carry the news to death row. With his partner, Bill Marsteller, he left immediately for the state capital to confer with Weaver about plans for another trial.

The court's decision was a victory for justice, the editor of the *Cleveland News* declared in apparent relief at the turn of events.

Thanks largely to the untiring efforts of two Cleveland attorneys, Nathan E. Cook and William Marsteller, Joe Weaver, a penniless colored man, will get a new trial on the charge of complicity in the murder of Jasper Russell, a watchman. *The News* is frankly gratified at this turn of events. Weaver may be equally as guilty as Alex Maynor, now serving a life term, who first testified against the former and then repudiated the evidence he had previously given. But the element of doubt in the minds of Weaver's loyal attorneys was shared by Chaplain Reed at the penitentiary. Criminal Judge Irving Carpenter of Norwalk, who presided at the trial, was also skeptical concerning the validity of the testimony which proved most damaging to Weaver's defense.

The setting aside of Joe Weaver's conviction by the state supreme court is a victory for justice. Full credit must go to Attorneys Marsteller and Cook for steadfastly maintaining the highest ethical principles of the bar. They have labored for their client at a great personal sacrifice.

The state can never make amends to Weaver for the horrors he has endured during his 22 months in the death house, if he should be exonerated. The least it can do at this time is to assure him a fair and speedy trial.[205]

By this time, Prosecutor Edward Stanton and his assistant, James Connell, had moved across the courtroom aisle to careers in vigorous defense of Cuyahoga County's accused.

Three days after the court's decision was handed down, Harry Smith announced the news to his constituency. He was unrestrained in his glee. "The Lord works in a mysterious way is an old and very familiar expression. He took Eddie Stanton and his crew out of the county prosecutor's office and then gave Joseph Weaver a new trial. Thank the Lord!"[206]

CHAPTER 13

OUT OF THE SHADOW

Finally, the letter Joe longed most to write appeared in the *Gazette*—the only one of his Editor Smith topped with a headline.

Weaver Thanks All

Dear Sir: By the help of God, through the voice of His people, He has answered our prayer by giving me a new trial. I know some who held special prayers for me, and thru the columns of your splendid paper, I wish to extend my profound gratitude to ALL who have stood so firmly for me and which has almost resulted in a victory. I have also written my thanks and appreciation to the State Supreme Court jurists for giving me another chance to prove that I am not a burglar nor a murderer. I hope to see you all soon.

With best wishes and kindest regards,
I am sincerely,

Joseph Weaver[207]

If the Black Hole of Cuyahoga County had changed at all, it had changed for the worse.

Cleveland News reporter Dan Gallagher had offered his judgment in the October 18, 1928 edition of the afternoon daily.

I have been a newspaper reporter for a good many years. In pursuance of my duties, I have visited scores of jails and prisons in various parts of the United States. Yesterday I spent seven hours in the Cuyahoga County jail at Cleveland. And among them all—north, south, east or west—it's the foulest shudder hole I ever set foot in….And after viewing it, I thank the Almighty it is not my lot—like many another—to be confined there as a material witness in some criminal case, innocent of wrongdoing, yet unable to supply bail. God help them; they are in a terrible plight….[208]

Four months after Gallagher's vitriolic article, Joe Weaver was escorted back to the jail, in keeping with the order of the state's highest court to return him to Cleveland.

"It's great to be back here," he said upon arrival on March 1st, on his way to a cell on "murderers' row."[209]

In the meantime, elsewhere in the city, supporters were emboldened by the court's reversal and mobilized on behalf of the man soon to be retried. Church leader Sydney Thompson called for a rally to raise money to reward Joe's attorneys for their tireless work. Harry Smith, though, cautioned his readers to wait for the outcome of the trial. He had only to bring up a recent rally that had turned into a fiasco at Mount Zion Congregational Church. Ward 11 Councilman Thomas W. Fleming, the first black person to serve in municipal government, had been indicted for bribery. Allegedly the official (who was sworn in as councilman-at-large in 1910 when only 8,500 Clevelanders were of African descent) had accepted $200 from a crippled former detective in exchange for introducing legislation in council to pay the ex-city employee's medical bills. Editor Smith reminded his readers that several prominent persons at the rally had expressed confidence in the councilman's innocence, but the masses had collectively voiced a wait-and-see opinion.

In short order, the councilman was convicted and went to prison maintaining he had done nothing wrong. Harry Smith was not willing to jump the gun a second time. Instructing his readers, the editor said:

When Joseph Weaver has been liberated will be the time for our people to raise money for his attorneys if they wish to. Not a dime should be given to any one for such a purpose until Weaver is at liberty. Then he can let our people know how much help he needs and the matter can be taken up and disposed of in a regular and well-organized way, the mass-meeting being held when the attorneys are presented whatever fund has been raised for them on the suggestion of Weaver.[210]

Marsteller and Cook were re-appointed by the court to defend Joe in the upcoming trial. Nate Cook was confident of victory and predicted to the newsmen that their client's case would not go to the jury provided the state did not call Alex Mayner to testify.

The state's key witness was brought back to Cleveland one month later. The old courthouse was a stone's throw from the dilapidated jail on the northwest corner of Public Square. The state still planned to use Mayner's testimony to bolster its case. In answer to a barrage of questions from the press, Alex said he was going to tell the court the same story he had told Chaplain Reed. He denied any knowledge of the murder and "what Weaver do."

Jury selection began April 1st, the day Alex arrived in Cleveland. Two days later, the panel paid a morning visit to the scene of the slaying.

While the legal machinery was getting into gear with the Defendant idling in county jail, one more letter was cranked out to Harry Smith.

Dear Sir: I hope you will pardon me for not having written you before now, as I did so often while in Columbus. One reason is that I have had nine times less time here to spend in writing than I had while in the death house in Columbus.

There have been many suggestions and propositions made to me since I have been here, pointing out the best and quickest ways to help me settle the debt to my attorneys, after I am liberated, if I am. Since I am on trial now, as you know, I have not made any arrangements or promises to any of them, and could not afford to do so before allowing you to be first choice as director for me. You played the fourth part of importance in my defense (attys Cook, Marsteller, Chaplain Reed and you) and I will look you up before I make a forward move with anyone other than my attorneys who have fought for me from the very first.

I have received *The Gazette*, regularly every week since I have been here as I did while in Columbus for the last thirteen months. I will be glad to do something to show my appreciation for the paper and the invaluable services you have rendered me in *The Gazette*, this year, and especially the Sunday you went from church to church in this city in zero weather, making speeches to help me. I hope you will receive this letter promptly. Many thanks to you as ever. I am,

Yours very truly,

Joseph Weaver[211]

From the first day of court, anxious backers of the man on trial crowded into the courtroom of Judge W. R. White, sitting on assignment from Gallipolis. No member of the Russell family was present.

On April 3rd, Assistant Prosecutor Edward J. Hopple opened the state's case in front of an all-white jury, equal in number of men and women. Hopple informed them that the state would rely on circumstantial evidence to convict the Defendant.[212]

The state called Don Kibbits to the stand. The Madison Avenue line motorman testified that the streetcar reached West 105th Street at 10:28 on the day of the murder. He said he saw two men running from the plant, but he could not say the Defendant was one of them.

The state then called for Jack Mansfield, another railway employee. Mansfield said on the stand that the car had stopped at that intersection between 10:30 and 10:40.

On cross-examination, Bill Marsteller forced the conductor to concede that the testimony two years earlier when he said the time was 10:30 was "more apt to be correct."[213]

Nate Cook introduced a letter in Mansfield's handwriting, addressed to the steel company and informing them he would "do everything he could to convict Weaver." The letter also made inquiry into his chances of obtaining a $1,000 reward offered by the company. The defense also introduced a copy of a letter sent Mansfield in reply stating that counsel for the company would make disposition of the reward in event of conviction.[214]

Alex Mayner's name was called. The state's witness spent the next two hours under fire from the assistant prosecutor, but would not take back his recantation when confronted with his testimony from the first trial. The diminutive man claimed he could not remember what he said back then. Under direct examination, the pivotal witness for the state denied making any of the statements read from the record. He further denied even any part in the crime. He claimed he was at home in bed that night, and with that passed out on the witness stand, sending the gallery into an uproar and the court into a recess. The witness came to himself ten minutes later.[215]

Without Alex Mayner's testimony, there was nothing to place the Defendant at the steel plant at the time Jasper Russell was killed. According to the morning newspaper:

> The phenomenon of perjury, now or past, left Assistant County Prosecutor E. J. Hopple helpless with his own witness. Maynor is already under a life sentence for the Russell murder and doesn't need to fear punishment for perjury....It was believed that Hopple would rest the state's case this morning.
>
> When he does, Defense Attorneys William F. Marsteller and Nathan E. Cook will demand a directed verdict of acquittal on the grounds that the circumstantial evidence against Weaver is insufficient to prove that he took part in the crime.
>
> [In opposition to what he had said at the first trial] yesterday, Maynor said that he only saw Weaver once on the day of the murder, at noon. Not only did he deny all other portions of the story, but he denied having given this fact in testimony at the previous trial.

> Common Pleas Judge W. R. White allowed the state to introduce parts of the transcript of the record of Weaver's first trial to "refresh Maynor's recollection, but he [Mayner] denied making any of the statements credited to him in the defense's transcript to testimony."
>
> Several state's witnesses were balked by the defense demand that a conspiracy between Maynor and Weaver be established to prove the competency of their testimony.[216]

Desperate to salvage its case, the state played its trump card. It called for Detective Lieutenant Frank Story with the intention of introducing through him Alex's original testimony.

That drew an objection from the defense table.

Judge White interrupted the verbal sparring to send the jury out. At the defense table Joe Weaver sat quietly, holding in his hand a tattered Bible.

The jurors were brought back in. The court refused to allow the detective to take the stand. The state had played its hand. Two words from the Bench trumped the state's case: "Objection sustained."

On the morning of April 5, 1929, William Marsteller threw down his biggest trump card when he motioned for a verdict of acquittal.

> Judge W. R. White ordered the not guilty verdict over the protest of Assistant County Prosecutor Edward Hopple.
>
> "I am not passing on Weaver's guilt or innocence. I am merely ruling that Ohio has been unable to introduce sufficient proof to warrant submitting this case to the jury.
>
> "I do not believe a word of the testimony given by Alex Maynor, but the state is helpless to do anything about it."
>
> Weaver hummed "There's a Rainbow Round My Shoulder," while the judge talked.[217]

The jurors retired to carry out the court's instructions and returned with a signed verdict. Hearing the judge announce the acquittal verdict, Nate Cook dashed across the courtroom and threw his arms around his wife. Reporters flocked to him and his equally exuberant partner. He and Marsteller said nothing more than, "We're well repaid for our two years of labor."[218]

> "Please wire my mother that I am free," were Weaver's first words after the directed verdict was ordered by the court. [He] received his first words of congratulations from an old white woman who had been in constant attendance at the trial during the week. Cook and Marsteller were besieged by a group of Weaver's friends. An old colored woman stepped forward and blessed the attorneys....
>
> Apparently dazed for a moment at the realization that he had been freed, Weaver burst into laughter as he left the courtroom and entered the corridor to leave the building.
>
> "I'm going to my home...to do some 'tall' thinking and get me a good meal," Weaver told a host of friends, many of them women in tears, as he entered the elevator.[219]

> Weaver emerged from Cuyahoga's murky County Jail at 11 yesterday morning....
>
> A throng of Weaver's friends blocked traffic at the jail corner of Public Square as Weaver came out "on the bricks" with Attorney Nathan E. Cook....
>
> "We prayed hard for you, Joe," girls in the crowd told Weaver as he edged his way through the crowd. "We're so happy...."
>
> "I'm going to look for a job, but I expect to preach the gospel," Weaver said as he departed.[220]

Ahead of them was Alex Mayner in shackles, with a guard to escort him on his return to Columbus. Joe, rejecting an offer from Alex, said to the onlookers:

> "Why should I shake his hand? He's luckier than I am.... I should have been free these last two years. He lied me into prison and saved his own life in the bargain."[221]

> At Cook's office, Weaver paused for a few moments and then remarked: "Well, now that I'm eligible, I guess I'll go get me a job soon."[222]

Almost immediately, the man soon to become a living legend was commissioned to write for one of the afternoon dailies. His article was headlined: "Weaver Writes Own Story; Freed in Murder, He Tells of Long Stay in Ohio Death House."

I awoke Saturday to my first day of freedom in twenty-five months. I was free of the charge of murder that threatened to send me to an early death for a crime that I knew nothing about. And I was free to go and come as I please and free to face the world knowing that I would have every chance to begin life anew.

To the ordinary man or woman this freedom means little. It is taken as a matter of course. But to me it is everything. I almost feel as if I have been called back from the grave.

My imprisonment began on March 15, 1927, two days after the killing of Jasper Russell, a night watchman at the Midland Steel Company.

Less than a month later, on April 11, to be exact, a jury of 10 men and two women found me guilty of the dreadful crime and the judge ordered my death in the electric chair on August 12.

At first I could hardly believe my ears. Faces of the jurors suddenly became blurred. I wanted to cry out against the injustice of it all, but the hand of a deputy sheriff, slipping handcuffs over my wrists, restrained me. I realized how futile that would be and followed him quietly from the courtroom to my jail cell.

Back there in my quiet cell I learned that injustice oftentimes brings a man friends he didn't know he had before. My two attorneys, Nathan E. Cook and William Fish Marsteller, came to me. They had been appointed to defend me by the court. Their work was finished when the jury returned its verdict. But they weren't going to desert me.

"Don't worry, Joe," they said to me. "We know you're innocent and we'll see that you get a square deal and get out of this."

Nothing, at the moment, could have made me happier. I knew that they would keep their promise and they've more than lived up to expectations. They couldn't have done more for me if I were their own brother.

Three days more in the county jail and I was taken to Columbus where they gave me a number, took away my personal belongings and gave me a cell in the death house.

Much has been written of this death house but I don't think it's ever been correctly described. There are two large cells and in the front of the cells a narrow passageway 12 feet long and three wide, where the prisoners are allowed to walk up and down an hour a day.

My cell was just over the spot where they used to have the death chair. The chair is now located directly behind my old cell but separated from it by a thick stone wall. You may wonder if I ever heard what went on in the death chamber when an execution was taking place. I couldn't, but I knew each of the prisoners well and I would lie on my cot and picture the scene as if it was right before me....

Most of these men were below average intelligence, several of them couldn't read or write, and I spent the greater part of my days writing to their friends and relatives....

You'll remember that Alex Maynor, whose testimony led the jury to find me guilty, told Chaplain Thomas O. Reed that I was innocent and wasn't even near the scene of the crime.

Then I was called before the clemency board and there heard Maynor repeat his statement as to my innocence. Now everything will be rosy, I thought. They'll surely let me go free.

I had yet to learn that when the law once gets you and finds you guilty, it isn't so easy to get off.

They took me back to my cell where I remained while my attorneys put their backs to the wall in my defense.

In those trying days immediately after my hearing before the board, I think I'd have gone crazy if I hadn't plenty to do. First of all, there were the letters to write for the condemned men, and then the guards made me a special watchman over a man by the name of John Braddock, [sic—Bradshaw] who killed a girl in Columbus.

John was nearly as big as I am. I'm six feet five and weigh over 200 pounds—and real tough, but I would handle him when he got real rough. Finally, he came to respect my strength and didn't cut up any more....

The glad news that I was to have a new trial in February came to me. I knew that I was soon to be free and felt a joy that cannot be surmised when we left Columbus for Cleveland on March 1.

The rest you know. What I'll do now that I'm free, I don't know. I'm looking for any kind of work, but I intend to go first to the Midland Steel Company, where I understand there's a job awaiting me.[223]

Now that the trial had ended to the satisfaction of the community, the time had finally come for the much talked-about rally. Three days after the acquittal, a throng showed up in a Monday evening celebration. Messiah Baptist Church was the chosen site. With money raised at Messiah and elsewhere, the exonerated man would be able to show gratitude to his indefatigable lawyers and visit his mother and other relatives in Georgia whom he had not seen in years. Hundreds of his supporters lifted their voices in faith-affirming hymns and spirituals. They also offered prayers of thanksgiving for their friend who no longer languished in the shadow of death.[224]

A choir of 100 voices from churches around the community responded to the hands of the local master of spirituals, Professor T. J. Hopson.[225]

Preachers and civic dignitaries lined the pulpit. Called upon to speak, they welcomed, thanked, and solicited the congregation on behalf of a man of no claim except the respect of his community and the evidence of a prayer-hearing God. When it was his turn at the rostrum, church leader Sydney Thompson said,

"It was the prayers of this poor boy's old mother down in Georgia, his tender-hearted, bent old mother, that brought him through. Through God, she has been given her boy back from death."[226]

Nathan Cook and William Marsteller being absent, a letter from them was read. It stated that they had only done their duty and under no circumstance wanted to share in any money given to Weaver.[227]

Finally, the long awaited speaker stepped up to the lectern in front of a packed auditorium. Before him were comforting faces of people like him with southern roots. The migration across the Mason Dixon had transformed sharecroppers into domestics, lawyers, and doctors, porters and plant workers and a public official or two. Knotty-veined hands gripped the light-streaked walnut stand to steady a massive frame. As was his practice, Joe had written down what he thought was important. With the notes in front of him, he began his speech with recognition of a trio of men. Men who had demonstrated character traits as uncompromising as black or white. He offered lavish praise for the court-appointed attorneys who went the extra mile for him. He profusely thanked Harry Smith for faithfully keeping him in touch with the outside world through the good "Old Reliable" *Gazette* while he was a prisoner. He spoke about his upbringing in Burke County and his conversion to Christianity. He unfolded the fate of the 13 men led away in his presence never to return. All this while his own execution loomed.

> Weaver, in [an] emotional voice that broke time and time again, told the story of his incarceration in Ohio penitentiary, of the horror of the shadow of the death chair, of his faith in God and the ultimate justice that he foresaw, and of the fight waged by Cook and Marsteller.[228]
>
> "Now to the young men and not only the young men. Let me advise you. You must think before you give a person your name and address for him to keep in his pocket and in your handwriting. I came 'in 48 hours of being killed because my name and address was found in a person's pocket, which I gave him for the purpose of selling him some cloth to make his wife a suit like the one I had sold him for himself."[229]

Prayer, the man declared, had brought him through the two-year legal battle. His untrained, distinct voice rolled on, strong and fervent, every declaration of unfaltering faith punctuated with a chorus of "Amen" and "Yes, Lord" from his down-home audience. The staccato of affirmations crescendoed from the pews as his testimony took on strength.

> "If I would attempt to tell you how I prayed, it would take as much speaking as I have done. God was my guardian as He was for Daniel in the lion's den. Nothing brought me through but faith like the faith of Abraham, and patience like the patience of Job."[230]

Then, over the long cries of exultation that filled the sanctuary, Joe Weaver finalized the whole matter:

> "Through many dangers, toils, and snares. I have already come. 'Twas grace that brought me safe thus far. And grace will lead me home."[231]

With that, Messiah erupted. A shout went up, three thousand strong as the man of conviction took his seat. Outside on Woodland Avenue, normally apathetic passersby were drawn to the church doors. They could hear voices singing a verse of "You Cain't Make Me Doubt Him," an old rhythmic, foot-stomping spiritual known to any Baptist with a taproot to Georgia, Alabama, or Mississippi.

> Then the congregation moved slowly down the close-packed church aisle to "shake hands with Joe" and to throw dollar bills into collection baskets that couldn't be emptied fast enough.
> They kept coming for more than half an hour, and the steady tramp of their feet set the two huge brass chandeliers in slow motion while huge shadows leaped from wall to ceiling to balcony....[232]

With the choir singing, Joe stood next to Messiah's rotund pastor, Boston J. Prince, at the collection table. An elderly woman, with the coins she dropped into the basket, also gave advice.

"Boy, go home to your family and friends. Go back to Georgia and make another start in life." Reject the North—this farce of a Promised Land—and its pretense at justice, she was saying.

"Don't tell him that," Pastor Prince said in rebuke. "Brother Weaver has done nothing wrong. An innocent, God-fearing man can live anywhere."

Other rallies took place in days to come. One at Shiloh Baptist Church where "Brother Weaver" was invited to speak and the basket was passed for him.

The Laymen's League "Weaver meeting" at Mount Zion Congregational Church on the next Sunday turned out to be "an unqualified success in every way," according to Roy Rector, president of the organization. In addition to the honoree, he presented such notables as Councilmen Clayborne George and Russell Brown, local NAACP branch president, Attorney Charles W. White, church leader Colonel Sydney Thompson, and Harry Smith. All spoke to an audience large in attendance, the *Gazette* owner's words of support as strong at the lectern as at his printing press.[233] Before long, the editor would spearhead efforts to put into Joe Weaver's pocket bigger bucks than the $88.41 raised that evening.

> If ever the great state of Ohio owed anybody anything, it surely is heavily indebted to Joseph Weaver, not only for the time lost in the penitentiary, but also for the mental suffering he sustained during that long period—something it is simply impossible to express in words, a most harrowing experience. The only wonder is that the man lived thru it all twenty-two months in the death-house at the penitentiary in Columbus awaiting electrocution, something simply nerve-wrecking to even contemplate....[234]

Zion Hill, Joe's home church, Shiloh, Liberty Hill, Triedstone, East Mount Zion, and Antioch—all Baptist churches—opened their doors to rallies that week. Quinn Chapel African Methodist Episcopal Church, a year or so later, hosted a South Side Republican Club meeting in support of state compensation for the wrongly imprisoned man.

By May 1929, Joe had enough funds to return to Georgia—not to stay, as ill-advised at Messiah earlier, but to visit his ailing 83-year-old mother in Midville. She had regained only half the weight lost during his confinement.

Before leaving for the South, though, there was one more letter to write. It was dated April 22, 1929, and addressed to the Governor of Ohio.

> Honorable Sir, Ever since I learned to read and read newspapers especially, and that has been for about the last twenty-five years, I have been reading about the gallows, scaffolds and the electric chairs and when certain ones died for certain crimes they committed, and sometime [sic] I would read that the last words the person who was executed said before the black mask was lowered over his face was gentlemen I am an innocent man. During those times I was not very much concerned about the persons executed and had no sympathy for them, and at the same time I did not believe it was possible that I could ever fall into such a predicament.

> On the 15th day of March 1927, I was picked up off the job while I was working and had a charge of first degree murder laid on me, and God knows Governor I had not anymore to do and knew not any more about the crime than you did.

> On April 15th 1927 I was pronounced guilty and the sentence of death was meted out to me by the presiding judge. On the 29th day of April 1927 I was taken to the death cell of the Ohio State prison and while there since I was in the best of hope of proving my innocence in a second trial I used part of my time experimenting. I decided since I have been reading for so many years that men dies in the electric chairs and gallows saying they are innocent, I am going to watch closely every one of these fellows and furthermore I am going to make it my business to pick them in a secret way and on the sly to find out how many innocent persons the States take the lives of.

> While I was there, there were about a half dozen men came in maintaining they were innocent of the crimes which they were

convicted of, and it did not take me over three weeks to the longest to find out their guilt—by they letting something fall by a slip of the tongue and catching themselves, and betraying them in their conversations.

I shook hands with 13 men who were executed during the 22 months I was incarcerated in the death house of Columbus, and I am well satisfied that—not one of those men was innocent because I sang and prayed and read and learned them the Bible daily. I told them day by day while conversing with them inspite of all you do don't die and go up before God with a lie in your mouth saying you are innocent if you are not because the Bible strictly tells you that all liars will have their part in a lake that burneth with fire and brim stone. They finally confessed to me because I held a Christian light for them.

Among the number which make fourteen, was John Sabo, a young Hungarian white man, he was put in the death cell two weeks before I was. I taught and learned him to read English, talk English, and write English. I wrote about 800 letters for him and read every letter he received for 20 of the months I was there. I learned him to read the English Bible and I stayed in the cell with him just he and I day and night [for] 22 months. I watched him as much as I did those other boys. He is no more related to me than any of the other seven white men I talked and stayed with.

John Sabo is white and I am colored. John Sabo is a Christian now, he read the Bible thru four times while I was there. Out of the fourteen men including John Sabo, he is the only one if the State of Ohio put to death I will be very doubtful that a guilty man was executed. I am convinced of Sabo's innocence. And Dear Governor if you were convinced of his innocence as I am you would pardon him because you do not want an innocent man in prison. I write please

Dear Governor to plead for clemency for John Sabo if that is the best you can do for him because I know the State of Ohio do not want to execute an innocent man.

I pray that you will be moved by Grace.

I am free now because I am an innocent man and my innocence has been proved and I expect to live a Christian upright life which will constrain other young men to follow after.

I am Yours very truly, (signed)

Joseph Weaver
2330 E. 57th St.
Cleveland, Ohio
22 months in death cell[235]

John Sabo was on schedule to die May 3, 1929. One week after the date of Joe Weaver's letter, Governor Myers Y. Cooper gave the 21-year old a sixty-day reprieve.

* * *

The tall black man stood respectfully at the casket with hat in hand. An eight-year life-changing chapter had come to a close. A final look at the hand that lay on the dead man's chest. It was the hand Joe Weaver would shake no more.

Years earlier, it was said of the City's Number One baseball fan:

When he dies and goes to the Happy Hunting Ground where all Home Teams win, the people of Cleveland probably will erect a monument just outside the Indians' baseball park and on it carve the words: "Nate Cook—He never quit rooting for Cleveland."[236]

(Should that happen, and Joe Weaver's daughter is not around, somebody scratch in this postscript: *And he never quit the fight for Joe Weaver.*)

The dark blue Lincoln rolled onto the upper level of the High Level Bridge. It was headed east into a future in freedom, northern style—a future that held marriage to a young widow with a toddler daughter, and the birth of Joe Weaver's only child.

Arguably, the Promised Land he had chosen was the best place for the former sharecropper from Georgia to thrive after all.

Radio drama, "Defenders of Democracy," 1941 photo. Left to right, William Marsteller, Joseph Weaver, Judge Julius M. Kovachy in the role of Nathan Cook, deceased.

[Twenty years earlier] Cleveland had built bridges to save time and money. The city also had learned that modern bridges not only promoted business, but helped to unify a municipality divided by great valleys.[237]

On the lower deck of the High Level Bridge, the connector of Cleveland east and west, a streetcar lumbered westward along strident 3,100 foot-long rails. Eventually it would arrive at West 106th and Madison Avenue. And Midland Steel.

EPILOGUE

In 1963, Joe Weaver went to Crile Veterans Hospital for a checkup. He had retired from the Hospital the year before, and looked forward to a chance to visit with old friends. At issue was the "heaviness" he said he felt on his chest at night when he slept. Jovial until half an hour before he died, he complained to a former co-worker that his stomach was upset. He told her he was going to return to his bed. Joe Weaver died there from a brain hemorrhage on July 15, 1963.

Susie Smith came from Georgia for her brother's funeral. She told me how she "prayed the locks off the jailhouse door."

Councilman Tom Fleming was paroled from the penitentiary in January 1933 after serving a little more than two years of a nearly three-year sentence. He returned to Cleveland still maintaining his innocence.

Later that year his citizenship rights were restored and he was reinstated to the bar.[238]

In 1957, Governor C. William O'Neill granted a Christmas commutation to 74-year-old Alex Mayner. In his trial Mayner had pled guilty to a lesser charge. The jury nonetheless found him guilty of first-degree murder while recommending mercy. Alex became eligible for parole when the first-degree murder charge was reduced to second degree by the Governor's action.[239]

Thirty-one years after he was convicted, Mayner was released from the Ohio Penitentiary on March 27, 1958.

William Marsteller retired from a notable career after 30 years of practicing law. In 1955, vacationing in Michigan he was stricken with acute appendicitis. He died on September 28, 1955, at 69, after an emergency operation.

Harry Smith, a bachelor, died suddenly in his office on December 10, 1941, and left no survivors. His property was left ultimately for the benefit of the Negro blind. At that point the *Gazette* was the longest publishing black weekly in the United States. True to its handle, the "Old Reliable" had never missed a Saturday publication date in 58 years.

I was fortunate to find a number of people with first- or second-hand knowledge of my father's ordeal. I found their names in the telephone directory. The first person located was Meyer Cook, in April 1986. Eighty years old, he was amazing with his immediate recollection of the case. Meyer explained that he had worked in his father's office as a 21-year-old assistant law director. Breathing laboriously, Mr. Cook told me he was terminally ill, but welcomed my questions and invited me to call back at any time. During May, we talked several times more. Meyer Cook died a month later.

Nathan Cook, Jr., was just as cooperative as his brother. He did not know any details of the case. He remembered, however, that Joe Weaver attended the wake at their home on Christmas Day of 1935. He suggested the route my father would have taken from the East Side, which was directly across the High Level Bridge.

I talked with William F. Marsteller, Jr., by phone. He knew nothing about the case, but shared anecdotes about his father and provided additional information through obituary articles.

It took a little more ingenuity to find the relatives of Jasper Russell. A newspaper ad strategically placed near Jasper's hometown drew a response in 1987. A letter came from Jasper's niece urging me to call at once. Evelyn Householder was puzzled by an inquiry into the 60-year-old Jasper Russell murder case. Our phone conversation, though, put her at ease. Evelyn was generous with her assistance, providing usable facts about the Russell family. Her uncle, William, invited me to his home in

Canton, Ohio. He showed me a picture of his brother Jasper and shared the few details he remembered about the case. For several years after that, I exchanged Christmas cards with him and his wife.

Ann Greene came forward in response to an appeal her pastor made from the pulpit one Sunday morning. Because one of the rallies was at Shiloh Baptist Church, I had called there asking if anyone remembered the Joe Weaver case. Ann was a youth attending the rally at Messiah Baptist Church with her mother. She provided the information about the conversation that took place around the collection table with the elderly woman. More importantly, though was the surprising fact that she also knew Orrie, who had changed her name to Irene. Irene had died a few years earlier and her widower was Leroy Parries, a deacon at Mount Sinai Baptist Church. I met him at his home. Leroy showed me a picture of the woman to whom he was married for 20 years. He also gave me names of Irene's relatives who might know something about the early years of her life. I learned about the miscarriages from Irene's niece in New Jersey.

Even more surprising was the finding of John Sabo. I called all the Sabos in the Akron directory. Only one responded affirmatively when asked was he about 80 years old. My next question was whether he was ever in Columbus. Cautiously he said yes. Then I asked the most important question: "Do you know a Joseph Weaver?"

"Yes," he said, with reticence.

I told the listener who I was and what I was doing; then I asked him again whether he remembered Joe Weaver. The reply rocked me.

"You're damned right I do. Your father was fourteen-karat gold!"

Mr. Sabo said he would be glad to talk with me, but wanted to wait until the weather had cooled off. The next month, September 1987, offered such weather. I drove down Interstate 77 to meet Mr. Sabo in a parking lot in Akron. A slightly built man was leaning on his car, arms folded and ankles crossed. Walking up to him, I looked for the twinkle in his blue eyes. Age had evidently robbed the blue of its brilliance. A coffee shop was nearby, but Mr. Sabo insisted that I follow him to his house. Sizing him up, I figured I could take the frail little guy if I had to.

Puzzled, I followed Mr. Sabo into the driveway of the house next to the address that I knew to be his. A young man stepped out the side door briefly. Mr. Sabo introduced his son, who then wished me well on my book. The old man led me across their adjoining backyards, a seamless, manicured carpet. We sauntered along the perimeter of his yard while he pointed proudly to his flower borders, fruit trees, and vegetable garden. The stroll ended at his back porch.

During the two hours that we talked, his blue eyes clouded over or brimmed with tears as painful memories surfaced. I felt compelled to apologize for the intrusion into his past. My host assured me that he didn't mind, because I was "not just anybody"; I was someone who could relate to what he had been through.

The interview got back on track. The aged man watched curiously as I took down some of his responses in shorthand. He was a deacon in the Catholic Church, he said proudly; an accomplishment that stemmed from my father's spiritual influence upon him.

"That's how I became a Christian," he said.

Asked about the tutoring experience, Mr. Sabo said that my father had helped him to learn English. He gave as an example how he was corrected in his pronunciation of the word *music*.

"Do you remember any of the songs he taught you?"

"I don't remember any *now*. My English was not too good at that time, you know. I would just sing what he told me. I didn't know what I was singing, but he was a good teacher."

I showed my host the carbon copy of the letter his former cell mate had written to the governor. Across the top of it, in Joe Weaver's handwriting was: *This letter is a copy of a plea I made to Governor Cooper in behalf of John Sabo which meant much in a commutation of his sentence to life.* (According to the *Cleveland Press* article of June 18, 1929, Mr. Sabo's prison sentence was commuted to life by Governor Cooper on that date.)

"He was a wonderful, wonderful man, your father was."

The last time that he saw his old cell mate, Mr. Sabo said responsively, was the day Joe left the prison for Cleveland and a second trial.

"What was that like for you?"

"It was a sad situation. He was leaving. I was being left behind."

Suddenly, the aged man wrested the reins of the conversation from me and accelerated its pace. His jaw tightened as he talked about his own case. He castigated the men he said had framed him. Men he had "lived to see die horrible deaths. Killed. Cancer. Things like that."

I asked him about the third degree. He too, he said, had been put through it.

"And, like your father, I never broke."

John Sabo was pardoned by Governor Frank J. Lausche on March 25, 1947, after 21 years of imprisonment. A few years later he married. He was a widower of 15 years when I visited him and met his son.

Tears welling up in his eyes, Mr. Sabo had one more thing to say to me just before I drove off. "Tell 'em in your book that that *nineteen-year-old kid* is still alive—and almost eighty."

*   *   *

To all of the people named above, I am deeply appreciative for the information they furnished that helped to flesh out this story. I am also grateful to all the churches and organizations named in the story—some of them still around after 75 years—for the support their members offered during my father's time of need.

Finally, I am glad that there was a *Cleveland Plain Dealer* reporter named Regine V. Kurlander. His Sunday feature article of September 14, 1930 in particular revealed the nature of Joe Weaver's character. I close *Conviction in Cuyahoga County* with the opening paragraphs of that article:

> Down in New York City the people stand in line at the box office in order to see a play called "The Green Pastures." They say Marc Connelly has done a [illegible word] job of depicting the

simple faith of the Negro and everyone flocks to see "God in his heav'n answering prayer."

Here in Cleveland at the Lamson & Sessions Co. a huge man sweats in the sun, shedding his overalls at night for a resplendent purple suit that hangs loosely on his six feet five. Seven o'clock finds him at choir meeting, and you hear his voice, now lusty, now crooning, "Steal away, steal away, steal away to Jesus."

The others are singing, too, but in the voice of Joe Weaver there is a triumphant note and a caress, almost as if there were a pact between him and the Lord.

For Joseph Weaver is free once more after having spent two years in the shadow of the death chair.

Preachers wrangle and scientists argue over the existence of God, but Weaver is just as sure as are those childlike characters of Connelly's that there is a supreme guide, and he's sure, he says, because God showed him his hand.

END NOTES

[1] Genesis 50:20, *The Bible: New International Version.*

[2] Roelif Loveland. *The Cleveland Plain Dealer*. November 16, 1933. © 1933. All rights reserved. Reprinted with permission.

[3] *The Gazette*, April 26, 1941.

    The state of Ohio paid about $12,000 to Joe Weaver and his attorneys, $2,000 of which went to Atty. Cook for traveling expenses to and from Columbus. The remaining $10,000 was split equally between the two attorneys and Joe.

[4] *The Cleveland Plain Dealer*, 1929. (Month and day unknown.)

    Also: Roelif Loveland. *The Cleveland Plain Dealer*, August 17, 1932.

[5] *The Cleveland Plain Dealer*, April 22, 1930.

[6] Owen L. Scott. *The Cleveland News*, April 22, 1930.

[7] *The Cleveland Plain Dealer*, May 3, 1930.

[8] Ibid.

[9] *The Cleveland Press*, April 22, 1930.

    Also: *The Cleveland Plain Dealer*, May 3, 1930—The report submitted by Attorney General Gilbert Bettman, First Assistant Attorney General Earl Shively and Special Counsels Joseph A. Godwon and Harry C. Levy, who with State Welfare Director H. H. Griswold conducted an inquiry on orders from Gov. Cooper, declared that: "We find the temporary lighting arrangements installed on the construction work on the date of the fire were improper and dangerous. Both as to type and manner of installation, and that they constituted the probable cause of the fire."

[10] *The Cleveland News*, April 27, 1930.

[11] *The Cleveland Plain Dealer*, April 22, 1930.

[12] Owen L. Scott. *The Cleveland News*, April 22, 1930.

[13] James H. Rodabaugh, editor. "Museum Echoes—The Ohio Penitentiary Fire." Vol. 32, No. 9, 1959, p. 68.

14 Ibid. (No page number)

15 Roelif Loveland. *The Cleveland Plain Dealer*, April 23, 1930.

Also: Ibid.

"You saw flames coming in at that time and refused to open the door?" Bettman asked, incredulously.

"When you're a guard, you're supposed to obey orders," the imperturbable Watkinson replied. "You got to obey orders or you'll probably get suspended."

A shudder went over the room.

Also: The Plain Dealer, May 3, 1930.

There is a conflict in testimony as to whether they had keys with them or whether it was necessary for them to return and make a second trip from the guard room to the G and H cell block. The distance from the guard room to the north end of the G and H cell block is about 350 feet.

When Little and Baldwin came to the cell block, they found Watkinson stationed at the cage gate leading from the floor of the cell house through to the steps that led to the upper ranges.

An altercation ensued at the gate. Watkinson refused to open the cage gate, claiming that Hall, captain of the night guards, who appeared about that time, had commanded him not to. For many minutes before this, shouting and cries to be released had been coming from the prisoners in the cell block.

Failing in their pleas, Baldwin and Little turned to unlocking the cells on the first range, and finally came back to Watkinson. Little claimed he grabbed the key from Watkinson's hand, and Watkinson claimed he opened the cage gate then, despite Hall's order.

Hall, after ordering Watkinson not to open the cage gate, proceeded to open the windows and then disappeared from the scene and took no further part.

16 *The Cleveland Plain Dealer,* April 23, 1930.

And last at the afternoon session came Capt. John Hall, ...who couldn't remember very well the things he had said and seen. But he did testify that, so far as he knew, he had given no orders to Watkinson telling him to keep the door locked, and that if he had said anything to him it had been something like this:

"Get the men out as quickly as you can."

Capt. Hall testified...that he didn't tell Watkinson anything about keeping the door shut; that the door, as a matter of fact, was open when he got there.

Also: The Cleveland News, April 22, 1930.

Testimony today indicated that guards were more intent on preventing a prison break than on saving the prisoners. Nobody seemed to have the keys. Nobody thought of the keys until it was too late. So the veteran warden, Preston E. Thomas, a man famed for his intelligent prison administration, was advised. They were dispatched. By that time axes and sledgehammers were being used to break open cells.

17 *The Cleveland News,* April 22, 1930.

18 *The Cleveland Plain Dealer*, April 22, 1930.

19 Ibid.

20 Ibid.

A prisoner claimed the day guard made this statement when begged to give up the keys. A dozen other prisoners corroborated him....

21 Kenneth Beall. *The Cleveland Press*, April 22, 1930.

Also: James H. Rodabaugh, editor. "Museum Echoes—The Ohio Penitentiary Fire." Vol. 32, No. 9, 1959, p. 68.

22 *The Cleveland Plain Dealer,* April 22, 1930.

23 *The Cleveland News,* April 27, 1927.

24 *The Cleveland News*, April 22, 1930.

25 *The Cleveland Plain Dealer*, April 22, 1930.

26 Owen L. Scott. *The Cleveland News*, April 22, 1930.

27 Roelif Loveland. *The Cleveland Plain Dealer,* August 17, 1932.

28 *The Gazette,* April 2, 1927.

That Zion Hill, organized in 1917, was already a sizable church is evidenced by the collection of $1,500 on March 26, 1927, reported in the *Gazette.*

29 Roelif Loveland. *The Cleveland Plain Dealer*, August 17, 1932.

30 *The Cleveland Press*, January 18, 1934.

31 J. D. Sayers. *The Gazette,* May 7, 1921.

32 Mellon, James. *Bullwhip Days—The Slaves Remember, An Oral History.* New York: Avon Books, 1990.

33 *The Gazette*, November 17, 1923.

34 *The Gazette*, January 29, 1921.

Also: Charles Reagan Wilson and William Ferris. *The Encyclopedia of Southern Culture, Vol. 1.* New York: University of North Carolina Press, 1989. pp. 306-307.

The Afro-American move from the South to the North, from country to city, and from farm to factory is one of the most significant social transformations in the history of the United States.

The settlement patterns of southern blacks, especially the compactness and segregation of the black community, encouraged the survival of southern culture. Racial segregation existed in the North as well as the South.

Also: Ibid. p. 317.

"Black newspapers are an invaluable reference if used properly. They sometimes provide the only evidence that a particular incident (especially protest) even occurred."

[35] Morris De Haven Tracy. *The Cleveland Press*, August 25, 1930.

[36] Charles Reagan Wilson and William Ferris. *The Encyclopedia of Southern Culture,* Vol. 1. New York: University of North Carolina Press, 1989. pp. 320-321.

[37] *The Gazette*, July 28, 1923.

[38] Charles Reagan Wilson and William Ferris. *The Encyclopedia of Southern Culture,* Vol. 1. New York: University of North Carolina Press, 1989. pp. 306-307.

[39] *The Gazette,* July 14, 1923.

[40] *The Gazette,* July 28, 1923.

[41] *The Gazette,* July 7, 1923.

[42] Ibid.

[43] *The Gazette*, May 15, 1926.

[44] *The Cleveland Plain Dealer*, December 24, 1935.

[45] *The Cleveland Press*, December 24, 1935.

[46] *The Cleveland Press*. No date. Some newspaper clippings, particularly from the *Press,* had no date stamped or only part of the date was legible, having faded with time.

[47] Hugh S. Fullerton. *The Cleveland Press*. No date.

[48] Ibid.

[49] *The Cleveland Plain Dealer*. December 24, 1930.

[50] National Commission on Law Observance and Enforcement, George W. Wickersham, chairman. *Report on Lawlessness in Law Enforcement*. Vol. IV, No. 11. Washington, DC: United States Government Printing Office, 1931, p. 119.

[51] Hopkins, Ernest Jerome. *Our Lawless Police—A Study of the Unlawful Enforcement of the Law*. New York: Viking Press, 1931, pp. 228-229.

[52] *The Cleveland Plain Dealer*, December 24. 1935.

[53] Roelif Loveland. *The Cleveland Plain Dealer*, November 5, 1932.

[54] *The Cleveland Press*, May 21, 1932.

[55] *The Cleveland Plain Dealer,* August 17, 1932.

[56] Ibid.

[57] *The Gazette,* August 6, 1921.

[58] *The Gazette,* November 14, 1921.

[59] *The Gazette,* August 6, 1921.

[60] *The Gazette,* January 23, 1926.

[61] *The Gazette,* June 12, 1926.

[62] *The Gazette,* August 4, 1923.

[63] Ibid.

[64] *The Gazette,* July 28, 1923.

[65] *Congressional Record—Sixty-Eighth Congress, first session.* "Just Pay for Postal Employees" Speech of Hon. Clyde Kelly of Pennsylvania in the House of Representatives. Friday, February 4, 1924, p. 10.

[66] Americanization Bulletin, Adult Education in Ohio. F. J. Heer Printing Company, Columbus, Ohio, 1923, pp. 24-25. Prepared by Ohio Department of Education, The Division of Americanization, 1923. Issued by the Cleveland Americanization Committee of the Mayor's War Board.

[67] Ibid.

[68] *The Cleveland Plain Dealer,* March 14, 1927.

[69] *The Cleveland Press,* March 14, 1927.

[70] *The Cleveland Plain Dealer,* March 15, 1927.

[71] *The Cleveland News,* March 15, 1927.

[72] *The Cleveland Press,* March 15, 1927.

[73] *Weaver v. The State of Ohio.* (No. 20861). Supreme Court of Ohio. *The North Eastern Reporter,* Vol. 165. February 20, 1929, pp. 571-572.

[74] *The Cleveland News,* March 15, 1927.

[75] Ibid.

[76] *The Cleveland News,* March 16, 1927.

[77] *The Cleveland Press,* March 16, 1927.

[78] *The Cleveland News,* March 16, 1927.

[79] Ibid.

[80] *The Cleveland Press,* March 17, 1927.

[81] Cuyahoga County Criminal Journal. *Report on the Condition and Management of County Jail.* Vol. 35 by Raymond Moley, pp. 461-463. Vol. 38 by John Lavelle, pp. 234-235.

[82] *The Cleveland Plain Dealer,* September 29, 1955.

[83] The Cuyahoga Bar Association. *Defenders of Democracy.* Cleveland: WHK Radio Drama, 1941.

[84] *The Cleveland News,* October 28, 1926.

[85] *The Cleveland Press,* November 13, 1922, and January 10, 1926.

86 *Weaver v. State of Ohio.* The State of Ohio, County of Cuyahoga §: In the Court of Appeals No. 8390. Brief, pp. 5-20. No date.

A brief is the trial attorney's written argument to the appellate court. It is not the full trial proceedings; the trial transcript was purged long before this book was written. Therefore, cross-examination of Joe Weaver and perhaps some other witnesses does not appear in the text.

87 Ibid. p. 8.

88 Ibid. p. 9.

89 Ibid. p. 10.

90 Ibid. pp. 10-11.

91 Ibid. pp. 11-14.

92 Ibid. pp. 14-17.

93 Ibid. pp. 17-18.

94 Ibid. pp. 18-19.

95 Ibid. pp. 19-20.

96 *Weaver v. State of Ohio. The North Eastern Reporter.* Vol. 165. February 20, 1929, p. 572.

97 *Weaver v. State of Ohio.* The State of Ohio, County of Cuyahoga §: In the Court of Appeals No. 8390. Brief, pp. 23-24. No date.

98 *The Cleveland Plain Dealer,* September 14, 1930.

Also: National Commission on Law Observance and Enforcement, George W. Wickersham, chairman. *Report on Lawlessness in Law Enforcement.* Vol. IV, No. 11. Washington, DC: United States Government Printing Office, 1931, p. 118.

In Cleveland, unlike Cincinnati, the third degree is prevalent. A judge reported that it was practiced constantly by the Cleveland police, and a former prosecutor said, "You can't overstate it."

Prolonged relay questioning is employed, with loss of sleep and deprivation of food and drink. Sometimes the prisoner is kept standing, clear of a wall, for many hours during the interrogation. If the prisoner starts to fall asleep while on his feet, he is wakened by slaps in the face. The questioning may also be accompanied by violence.

There is evidence of the beating of prisoners over the kidneys and the soft hollows above the hips with a weapon such as a rubber hose or a sausage-shaped sandbag made of silk, these instruments being chosen because, when properly applied, they leave no marks. It is said that the prisoner is frequently struck from behind so that he may not see the person who hit him, and as a result will be unable to identify him in court.

99 *The Cleveland Press,* April 13, 1927.

[100] *Weaver v. State of Ohio. The North Eastern Reporter*, Vol. 165. December 17, 1928, p. 570.

[101] Ibid.

[102] Ibid. pp. 570-571.

[103] *Weaver v. State of Ohio.* The State of Ohio, County of Cuyahoga §: In the Court of Appeals No. 8390. Brief, pp. 48-49. No date.

[104] Ibid. pp. 51-52.

[105] Ibid. pp. 25-26.

[106] Ibid. p. 26.

[107] Ibid.

[108] Ibid. pp. 26-27.

[109] Ibid. p. 27.

[110] Ibid. p. 28.

[111] Ibid.

[112] Ibid.

[113] Ibid. pp. 28-29.

[114] Ibid. p. 29.

[115] Ibid.

[116] Ibid.

[117] Ibid. p. 30.

[118] Ibid.

[119] Ibid.

[120] Ibid. p. 32.

[121] Ibid. pp. 30-35.

[122] Ibid. p. 36.

[123] Ibid. p. 37.

[124] Ibid. p. 39.

[125] Ibid. pp. 53-54.

[126] Ibid. pp. 42-45.

[127] *The Cleveland News,* April 8, 1929.

[128] *The Cleveland News,* April 16, 1927.

[129] *The Cleveland Press,* April 23, 1927.

[130] *The Cleveland Plain Dealer*, April 27, 1927.

[131] Cuyahoga County Criminal Journal, Vol. 43, p. 339.

[132] Regine V. Kurlander, *The Cleveland Plain Dealer,* September 14, 1930.

[133] Letter dated May 4, 1927, written by the National Urban League's Executive Secretary.

[134] *Weaver v. State of Ohio.* The State of Ohio, County of Cuyahoga §: In the Court of Appeals No. 8390. Brief, p. 2. No date.

[135] Ibid. pp. 3-4.

[136] Ibid. p. 45.

[137] Ibid. p. 49.

[138] Ibid. pp. 50-51.

[139] Ibid. pp. 52-55.

[140] Ibid. p. 56.

[141] Ibid. p. 62.

[142] Regine V. Kurlander, *The Cleveland Plain Dealer,* September 14, 1930.

[143] Ibid.

[144] Ibid.

[145] Fornshell, Marvin E. *The Historical and Illustrated Ohio Penitentiary: A Complete Work on the Big Prison: All Departments, Escapes, Executions by Hanging and Electrocution, Punishments, Rules, etc.* Fully Described by Marvin E. Fornshell. Columbus, Ohio, Marvin E. Fornshell, 1903, 1906.

[146] Regine V. Kurlander, *The Cleveland Plain Dealer,* September 14, 1930.

[147] Ibid.

[148] *The Cleveland News,* April 8, 1929.

[149] Ibid.

[150] Regine V. Kurlander, *The Cleveland Plain Dealer,* September 14, 1930.

[151] *The Cleveland News,* April 8, 1929.

[152] *The Cleveland News,* January 11, 1928.

[153] *The Cleveland Plain Dealer,* January 15, 1928.

[154] Letter to Ohio Governor A. Vic Donahey. From Joe Weaver's prison file at the Ohio Department of Rehabilitation and Correction, Columbus, Ohio. No date.

[155] Ibid.

[156] *The Gazette,* January 21, 1928.

[157] *The Cleveland Plain Dealer,* September 14, 1930.

[158] *The Cleveland Plain Dealer,* January 15, 1928.

[159] Ibid.

[160] *The Cleveland News,* January 15, 1928.

[161] *Weaver v. State of Ohio.* State of Ohio, County of Cuyahoga §: In the Court of Appeals No. 8390. Columbus, 1928. Brief of Plaintiff in Error. Office of the Board of Clemency.

[162] *The Gazette,* January 28, 1928.

163 *Weaver v. State of Ohio. The North Eastern Reporter*, Vol. 166. December 17, 1928 (No number on the original), p. 595.

164 Davis, Russell H. *Memorable Negroes in Cleveland's Past.* Western Reserve Historical Society: Cleveland, Ohio, 1969, p. 33.

165 *The Cleveland News,* 1928. (Month and day undetermined)

166 *The Cleveland News,* February 1, 1928.

167 *The Cleveland News,* February 2, 1928.

168 *The Gazette,* October 2, 1926.

169 *The Gazette,* March 17, 1928.

170 The Cuyahoga Bar Association. *Defenders of Democracy.* Cleveland: WHK Radio Drama, 1941.

171 *The True Citizen,* February 18, 1928.

172 Letter to Ohio Governor A. Vic Donahey. From Joe Weaver's prison file at the Ohio Department of Rehabilitation and Correction, Columbus, Ohio. No date.

173 *The Gazette,* April 7, 1928.

174 *The Gazette,* March 31, 1928.

175 *The Gazette,* May 26, 1928.

176 *The Gazette,* September 22, 1928.

177 Dan Gallagher. *The Cleveland News,* October 15, 1928.

178 *The Cleveland Plain Dealer,* May 27, 1926.

179 *The Cleveland News,* October 30, 1928.

180 *The Gazette,* November 24, 1928.

181 *The Cleveland News,* 1928. (Month and day unreadable.)

182 Regine V. Kurlander, *The Cleveland Plain Dealer,* September 14, 1930.

183 *The Cleveland Plain Dealer,* November 30, 1928.

184 *The Gazette*, December 15, 1928.

185 *The Gazette,* January 12, 1929.

186 *The Gazette,* January 19, 1929.

187 *The Gazette,* January 12, 1929

188 Ibid.

189 Letter to Ohio Governor A. Vic Donahey. From Joe Weaver's prison file at the Ohio Department of Rehabilitation and Correction, Columbus, Ohio. December 24, 1928. Dates from January, 1928, to January, 1929.

190 *Ibid.*

191 *The Cleveland News,* December 13, 1928.

This last appeal, now pending before the appellate court, is based on section 13746 of the Ohio code which states that the "application for a new trial shall be by motion, filed at the term verdict is rendered, and, except for the cause of newly discovered evidence material for the person applying, which he could not, with reasonable diligence, have discovered and produced at the trial, shall be filed within three days after verdict is rendered unless unavoidably prevented."

The comma was omitted after the word "trial" in a test case of this section years ago. Interpreting the law from that case, courts ever since have held that a man convicted of a crime cannot obtain a new trial unless it is requested within the same term of court in which conviction was had.

[192] *The Gazette,* January 5, 1929.

[193] *The Cleveland News,* December 28, 1928.

[194] Arthur Brisbane, *The Cleveland News,* December 25, 1928.

[195] *The Gazette*, January 15, 1929.

[196] *Weaver v. State of Ohio. Sabo v. Same.* (Nos. 21473, 21483) Supreme Court of Ohio. *The North Eastern Reporter,* Vol. 165. February 27, 1929, p. 574.

The sole question presented is whether or not the court of common pleas has jurisdiction in a criminal case, after conviction, to entertain a motion for a new trial upon the ground of newly discovered evidence, filed at a term subsequent to the one in which the verdict was rendered.

(1) Criminal procedure in this state is regulated entirely by statute, and is found in part 4, tits. 1 and 2, of the Code of Criminal Procedure (sections 12368 to 13764, General Code, inclusive). The section of the Code under consideration is 13746, which provides as follows: "The application for a new trial shall be by motion, upon written grounds, filed at the term the verdict is rendered, and except for the cause of newly discovered evidence material for the person applying, which he could not, with reasonable diligence, have discovered and produced at the trial, shall be filed within three days after the verdict was rendered unless unavoidably prevented."

The construction of the section of the General Code in question has been before the lower courts of this state, including the circuit court and the Court of Appeals, upon several occasions, as to the right to grant a new trial for newly discovered evidence, when the application is made after the term at which the verdict is rendered....

(2, 3) In all the cases we have been able to find in the courts of this state, the universal construction of the statute in question is that the courts are without jurisdiction to grant a new trial for newly discovered evidence, filed after the term at which the verdict was rendered. It seems to be the policy of the law that the matter shall be concluded by the action taken at the term. If a motion could be filed after term, it might be filed at any time, no matter how remote from the time of the trial, after the state's witnesses have disappeared, or been scattered, or, perhaps died, so that the state might be at a great disadvantage in a new trial....

Our opinion is that the courts below were right in reaching the conclusion that, under the statute, section 13746, General Code, the trial courts were without jurisdiction to grant a new trial on the ground of newly discovered evidence when the motion therefor [*sic*] was filed at a term subsequent to the one at which the verdict was rendered. The judgments of the courts below in both cases will therefore be affirmed.

Judgments affirmed. p. 574.

197 *The Gazette,* January 26, 1929.

198 *The Gazette,* February 16, 1929.

199 *The Gazette,* February 2, 1929.

200 *Weaver v. State of Ohio. The North Eastern Reporter.* Vol. 165. Supreme Court of Ohio. February 20, 1929, p. 571.

201 Ibid. p. 572.

The right to cross-examine a witness does not extend beyond the subjects inquired of by the party offering the witness and the subjects the party offering the witness was entitled to but did not inquire about. The defendant at the trial did not inquire as to the declarations of the 5 year old child, and was not entitled to inquire as to such declarations. The fact that the state was erroneously permitted to inquire of such declarations furnishes no foundation upon which to base the introduction of further incompetent evidence. Aside from the incompetence of the evidence elicited from the witness Bedell on cross-examination, the ground laid for the impeachment was at the central police station and not at the rooming house of the witness Bedell, and did not entitle the state to introduce evidence of a conversation at the rooming house: and, aside from that, even though the foundation had been laid at the rooming house, the right to impeach extended only to the remark which the witness testified she made or denied that she made.

The inquiry of the witness Bedell was as to a declaration of a child who did not testify, and was too young to testify, and, being neither a part of the res gestae, nor made in the presence of the defendant, was purely hearsay. The impeaching testimony of witness Jacobs was tinctured with the same vice.... pp. 572-573.

202 Ibid. p. 573.

203 *The Gazette,* February 23, 1929.

204 *The Cleveland News,* February 21, 1929.

205 *The Cleveland News,* February, 1929. (day not clear)

206 *The Gazette,* February 23, 1929.

207 *The Gazette,* March 9, 1929.

208 Dan Gallagher. *The Cleveland News,* October 18, 1928.

209 *The Cleveland News,* March 1, 1929.

210 *The Gazette,* March 15, 1929.

[211] *The Gazette,* April 13, 1929.

[212] *The Cleveland News,* April 3, 1929.

[213] *The Cleveland News,* April 5, 1929.

[214] Ibid.

[215] Ibid.

[216] The *Cleveland Plain Dealer,* April 5, 1929.

[217] The *Cleveland Press,* April 5, 1929.

[218] *The Cleveland News,* April 6, 1929.

[219] Ibid.

[220] *The Cleveland Plain Dealer,* April 6, 1929.

[221] Ibid.

[222] *The Cleveland News,* April 6, 1929.

[223] Joseph Weaver. *The Cleveland News,* April 8, 1929.

[224] *The Cleveland News,* April 9, 1929.

[225] *The Chicago Defender,* April 13, 1929.

[226] *The Gazette,* April 13, 1929.

[227] *The Cleveland News,* April 9, 1929.

[228] Ibid.

[229] *The Gazette,* April 13, 1929.

[230] Ibid.

[231] Ibid.

[232] *The Cleveland Plain Dealer,* April 9, 1929.

[233] *The Gazette,* April 20, 1929.

[234] *The Gazette,* March 7, 1931.

[235] Carbon copy of a typewritten letter to the governor of Ohio.

Seven days after the letter, Philip W. Porter of the *Cleveland Plain Dealer*'s Columbus bureau offered a report. It appeared in the *Plain Dealer* on April 30, 1929 under the headline: Hear Governor May Save Sabo.

For more than two years, John Sabo, Hungarian youth who once toiled in an Akron rubber factory, has paced the death cell at Ohio Penitentiary, hoping and praying…. He now faces electrocution Friday. The young man whom thousands believe innocent and for whom such a determined fight is being made by his friends and countrymen, may not have long to fret, for reports are beginning to come from usually reliable sources that Gov. Myers Y. Cooper will commute his sentence within the next two days.

One thing fresh in the minds of the chief executive and his advisers is the recent case of Joseph Weaver, Cleveland colored man, who sat in the death cell for month after month, as Sabo has done, hoping and trusting, and finally became a free man….

Last week, the Board of Clemency heard two new witnesses say that Sabo did not kill Barton C. Painter of Akron. A. S. Weidenfeldt, a junk dealer, testified that he saw a tall, slim man running away after the murder. Sabo is short and stocky, and Weidenfeldt said it could not have been he. Mrs. Anna Kovacs of Akron said that Sabo did not commit the murder and accused one of the witnesses who testified against him. Sabo with tear-filled eyes, stoutly maintained his innocence to the Plain Dealer correspondent today.

"All I can say is that I am innocent," he said. "I never knew the man who was killed. I had never seen him until after the trial somebody showed me his picture. I don't know how I came to be arrested, except that some people I thought were my friends framed me.

"All I can do is to keep up my courage and have faith in God doing right by me. It is bad enough to stay here two years when I have done nothing wrong."

[236] Hugh S. Fullerton. *The Cleveland Press.* No date.

[237] William Ganson Rose. *Cleveland: The Making of a City.* Cleveland: World Publishing Company, 1950, p. 681.

[238] *The Cleveland Plain Dealer,* August 24, 1933.

[239] *The Cleveland Press,* December 24, 1957.

Give the Gift of

CONVICTION
IN CUYAHOGA COUNTY
to Your Friends and Colleagues

CHECK YOUR LEADING BOOKSTORE OR ORDER HERE

❑ **YES**, I want _____ copies of *Conviction in Cuyahoga County* at $14.95 each, plus $4.95 shipping per book (Ohio residents please add $1.59 sales tax per book). Canadian orders must be accompanied by a postal money order in U.S. funds. Allow 15 days for delivery.

❑ **YES**, I am interested in having Jo Jo Weaver speak or give a seminar to my company, association, school, or organization. Please send information.

My check or money order for $_____ is enclosed.
Please charge my ❑ Visa   ❑ MasterCard
                   ❑ Discover ❑ American Express

Name_____

Organization _____

Address _____

City/State/Zip _____

Phone_____ E-mail _____

Card # _____

Exp. Date_____ Signature _____

Please make your check payable and return to:
House of Jabez
16781 Chagrin Blvd., #247 • Shaker Heights, OH 44120
Call your credit card order to: 800-484-8147 (code 5894)
or 216-751-9343
Fax: 216-751-0112
www.convictionincuyahoga.com